The Pastor's CHURCH GROWTH HANDBOOK

EDITED BY DR. WIN ARN

PUBLISHED BY
Church Growth Press

THE INSTITUTE FOR
AMERICAN CHURCH GROWTH

Published by Institute for American Church Growth
150 South Los Robles, #600, Pasadena, CA 91101

Printed in U.S.A.

Library of Congress Catalog Card No. 79-52954
ISBN 0-934408

Contents

gratis

65097

Introduction

"It's here!" Finally, a handbook that covers the spectrum of church growth and puts it at your fingertips.

Would you like some ideas on motivating your laity for outreach? It's here! How about ways to reach your ethnic neighbors? It's here! Are you interested in the characteristics of growing churches? It's here!

In the following pages are gathered what we believe to be some of the outstanding articles and contributions of the church growth movement focused on the American scene.

Thanks to the pace-setting church growth magazine, **CHURCH GROWTH: AMERICA**, insights from America's foremost growth authorities are offered to you in this volume. Compiled over the last two years, this *Pastor's Church Growth Handbook* brings you up to date on what's happening in church growth.

Regular subscribers to **CHURCH GROWTH: AMERICA** are continuing to grow through the insights of this important magazine. If you are not one of the many pastors or executives receiving this important leadership tool, subscribe today and don't miss another issue of some of the most essential information available today on how to grow a church.

Church Growth...an exciting approach to seeing your church become all it was created capable of becoming...reaching out and winning people...making disciples and responsible church members. Expanding new horizons. Christians enthusiastically involved in the ministry and outreach of your church.

Come join the celebration!

How to Find a Pastor Who Fits Your Church ...or How to Find a Church That Fits You

BY DR. WIN ARN

The Pulpit Committee was in disarray! Nine months of meetings, dozens of candidates later, the pulpit was still empty! Members of the congregation wanted action! The Committee had prayed...interviewed candidates...contacted denominational headquarters...but the church was still without a pastor.

Every church periodically faces the problem and challenge of calling a pastor—a strategic decision for the life and growth of that church. A "right" decision could bring health, vitality and growth; a "wrong" decision could bring disharmony, stagnation and decline. Of course, every church wants to make the "right" decision. So does every pastor!

Let's assume that our Pulpit Committee represents a church committed to carrying out the Great Commission...reaching its community for Jesus Christ...and growing. In seeking a new pastor, a church will look for

Dr. Win Arn is President of the Institute for American Church Growth, Pasadena, California.

certain qualifications; and the pastor, committed to the Great Commission...to making disciples...to church growth, will look for certain qualities in the church.

A survey of pastors and churches across America reveals all shapes, sizes, personalities and ministry styles. God does not have a preconceived notion of the "perfect pastor" from which he makes all models and versions. Nor does God seem to have one mold He labels "perfect church." Pastors and churches come in infinite varieties—as broad as human personalities, as diverse as human needs, as inclusive as the purposes of God.

The intricate mosaic of people and cultures requires churches and pastors to fit together, to complement each other, to support each other. Frankly, some pastors and churches simply do not "mix," through no real fault of either.

Yet, if we believe that His Body—the Church—functions as a living, dynamic organism, where each sinew and cell has its particular place and function, then we must conclude that God has the right man for the right church and the right church for the right man. The problem—getting the two together!

Certainly divine guidance is needed. The spiritual disciplines of prayer, seeking His will, being led of His Spirit are of prime importance. Are there additional considerations? I think so.

1. FITTING THE HOMOGENEOUS GROUP

In growing churches, the pastor fits the homogeneous group. The term "homogeneous" is part of the classic Church Growth vocabulary. It simply describes a group of people where all the members have some characteristics in common and feel they "belong," that they are part of the fellowship, where they like one another and share similar interests and culture.

Research clearly indicates that churches grow, and grow

best, in their own homogeneous units. Churches develop their own individuality and active members generally fit the same patterns. People want their pastor to be "like" them. Not too far above or below, not too far ahead or behind.

When a pastor *establishes* a church, the homogeneous group will be his kind—for his kind of people are the ones who will be attracted. However, when a pastor is called to an established church, he enters a homogeneous group which is already formed and is usually fairly rigid in structure. A homogeneous group has many dimensions. It may include one's educational, ethnic, social, economic or cultural background, or a combination of these elements which combine to make us what we are. In God's sight there is no more merit in being the pastor of a large church than of a small church...of a rich church than of a poor church...of a sophisticated church than of a common church. Yet, in man's sight there are differences. The important consideration for a successful ministry is that the pastor and the church fit the same basic homogenous unit.

A church must also be aware of a potential "homogeneous problem." For, while a church grows best in its own group, it can also die there by becoming an "exclusive club" or a small "clique" where it has sealed itself off from people in its community. "Why grow? We like it like it is," represents an attitude which will immediately stop the growth of any church and in time produce decay and death.

2. ANTICIPATING A LONG MINISTRY

As a church growth consultant, I know of very few growing churches with high rates of pastoral changes. Such churches in fact are often declining ones. I recently conducted a study of 58 churches in the Pacific Southwest. Of these 58 churches, over three-fourths of them had had a pastoral change in the last three years. And a high percentage of these churches were plateaued or declining. Throughout, there was a mentality, almost expectancy, that the pastor would be here today and gone tomorrow. The people expect the pastor to have a short ministry...and he does! With such attitudes, no firm commitments are made...no close relationships established...no long range plans developed.

How many pastors see their call as a stepping stone until their "real talents" are discovered by a bigger, better church?

If the church and pastor were to look upon their relationship as an irrevocable commitment, a marriage that vows "'till death do us part," the dynamics would be totally different. There would be problems, but they would become stepping stones rather than stumbling blocks to extended commitments and growth. The value of a long-term commitment in marriage, or in a pastor-church relationship, has great effect on a growing, positive ministry.

3. INVOLVING THE LAITY

Basic assumptions of both pastor and church are of great importance. A church that feels, "We pay our staff to do the work for us," is doomed to failure. Likewise, the pastor who takes upon himself the authority for all decisions, planning, and implementation will flounder in frustration. Research is conclusive on this point—if a church is serious about the Great Commission, involving the laity is of utmost importance. *The growth of a church is uniquely dependent on the laymen.* The pastor who sees his role as an enabler to help the laity discover and utilize their unique gifts is far ahead of the pastor who tries to "run the whole show."

The use of gifts and involvement of the laity is far more than the maintenance of the existing body. Using gifts in ministry and outreach is an essential ingredient to a healthy, growing church. I discussed the issue with Dr.

Donald McGavran, world church growth authority, recently. "Do you believe," I asked, "that in a congregation there are gifts for the growth of the church?" McGavran responded "You would misuse God's gifts if you used them solely for the service of existing Christians. As we see God's overwhelming concern for the salvation of men, we must assume that His gifts are given to men, in a large part, that the lost may come to know Him, whom to know is life eternal."

In our Church Growth Seminars, a portion of the time is given to analyzing how a church uses its lay leadership. Church growth students analyze church leadership in five different classes:

Class I Leadership: members in the church whose energies primarily turn inward toward maintenance of the organizational structure of the church.

Class II Leadership: members in the church whose energies primarily turn outward toward the non-Christian community in an effort to bring them into the body of Christ.

Class III Leadership: members in the church who are partially paid and whose activities are divided between the church and outside activities.

Class IV Leadership: individuals in the church who are full time paid personnel viewed as professional staff.

Class V Leadership: denominational, district and/or administrative personnel, usually removed from the immediate scene of the local church.

The key to dynamic, effective church growth is to be found in the recruiting, training and utilizing of Class II workers.

A bar graph, based upon actual numbers of people involved as Class I and Class II leaders, helps most churches immediately perceive that the wealth of their energies, efforts, and finances is devoured in maintenance of the church in Class I efforts.

4. UTILIZING TIME

Remember, our church looking for a new pastor is concerned with the Great Commission, with winning its community, and with *growth*. How a pastor uses his time has great effect on the growth of his church. Because the pastor is not supervised, he must determine the areas of greater and lesser importance and decided how much time he should allot to each. Unfortunately, many churches, in choosing a pastor, place greatest priority on the man's ability to preach. Certainly congregations are entitled to prepared and well-delivered messages. Yet, sermon delivery represents a very small portion of the pastor's total work week. Indications are that the sermon, by itself, is a relatively minor factor in the growth of the church. How then should a pastor spend his time to have the greatest effect in church growth?

Broad areas of responsibilities a pastor must include in his time schedule are: sermon preparation, reading and studying, counseling, visitation of members, administrative duties, attending meetings, visitation of prospective members, and training laity for outreach. Which of these areas should be emphasized if the church is to grow?

In researching this question, evidence to date indicates a significant correlation between two of these variables and a growing church: the pastor who spends a high proportion of time visiting prospects and training laity for outreach tends to have a church with significant growth.

5. VISION FOR GROWTH

"Church Growth Eyes" is a term used by those fluent with church growth vocabulary in referring to individuals and churches who have developed a sensitivity to "seeing the possibilities and applying appropriate strategies to gain maximum results for Christ and His Church." A pastor...and a church...with this type of vision make a winning combination.

Church growth results are achieved because some individuals—pastor or laymen—see with church growth eyes the possibilities God has for their church and then determine to achieve these goals. Such people are not satisfied with doing the "busy work" of the church. For them, God's desire is for non-Christian people in their community to find Jesus Christ...to become disciples and responsible members of the church. That's Church Growth! Such visions for growth usually involve "leaps of faith."

Some years ago, when making a film entitled "Circus" with a group of young people, we were waiting for the cameraman to return with film. The circus paraphernalia was all around us in the large arena. During performances, the finale of the program was a trapeze act by skilled young people on the high bars.

In the boredom of the moment, one of the youths turned to me and pointing to the bars said, "Why don't you try it?" I quickly tried to change the topic, but other youths soon began the chorus, "It's easy. You'll like it. Try it." It was put up or shut up. Climbing up the small rope ladder, I passed the net which looked very wide and secure...higher... higher...20 feet...30...40...45 feet...50 feet...Crawling onto a small platform, I looked down and saw the safety net had shrunk considerably...yet the youths urged me on. Swaying in the breeze, I mustered all my courage, took a hardy grip and finally went swinging out into empty space, seeking the second bar which had been released for me. Out there, alone, I immediately made three discoveries! While I wasn't thinking about church growth at the time, they relate directly to a leap of faith.

First, one cannot hold onto the old bar with one hand while reaching out to grab the new one. A definite commitment, "letting go" with both hands, is necessary to fly through the air and reach the goal.

Second, you do not have forever to make up your mind!

Third, it is a frightening experience to let go of one's security.

If a church is to grow, it needs both a pastor and individuals who will take "leaps of faith," letting go of their securities and reaching for new heights. Bold pastors, visionary churches, committed Christians. These combinations make for successful growing churches.

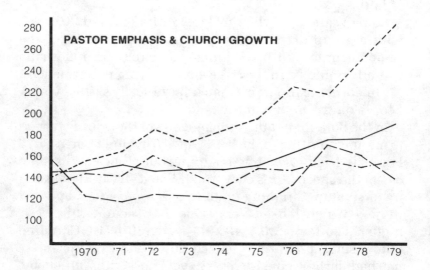

PASTOR EMPHASIS & CHURCH GROWTH

This graph represents the membership of four essentially identical churches over a 10 year period. The "independent variable" was the emphasis each pastor placed on his activities within the church.

-------- Visiting prospective members & training laity for outreach
———— Counselling and visitation of members
— — — Administrative duties   Attending meetings
—·—·—· Sermon preparation & reading/studying

Sheep Stealing and Church Growth

BY DR. DONALD McGAVRAN

One of the most common explanations for growing churches by other churches (or denominations) is that they "steal sheep." We have heard this claim across the United States, and all around the world. Sometimes the charge is leveled against the Pentecostals or the Seventh Day Adventists, or even Roman Catholics. What, really, is the substance of this allegation?

The fact is that millions of neglected Christians live all around us. Any pastor who runs an attractive, aggressive program will pull some of these neglected people away from their home churches. The process goes on all the time. When a member disagrees with his fellow members, board, or minister, he often stops coming and joins another church. Or, a neighbor may say to Mrs. T., "Do visit our church. We have such a lovely choir and such warm fellowship." As the friendship develops, Mrs. T. drops out of her old church and becomes a member of the other. This coming and going is a perpetual process.

Dr. McGavran is Chairman of the Board of the Institute for American Church Growth.

On the whole it is a good thing. People ought to be free to worship God where they wish to and churches ought to serve their members well. When the standard of service gets low, members leave and go to other churches. Automatic pruning helps keep churches active and dutiful. The pastor does not want a captive audience, which has to take whatever he gives. It keeps the pastor on his toes to know that while he is free to preach the Word as he sees it, his people are also free to worship elsewhere if they feel he is unbiblical or not challenging enough.

The Church has much to gain and little to lose by maintaining that the only thing which should keep a member from worshipping in this congregation, rather than in some other, is personal choice. Religious freedom is precious and easily lost. Opposition to this view is fathered by the State Churches of Europe. In these, men and women **belong** to the Church in the same way that peasants belong to the feudal lord. They were **born into this** Church, be it Lutheran, Presbyterian, Anglican, or Roman Catholic. It was sinful (so they were taught) to later join another denomination. Any pastor who tried to attract them was sheep stealing.

Freedom of religion and conscience simply did not exist. Being baptized in infancy was like calves being branded—from then on they **belonged** to this Church and woe betide him who took them into another.

The picture is complicated by the fact that as different understandings of biblical faith developed, different views were preached, often with fiery vehemence. The Millerites, believing that the Lord would return on Oct. 22, 1844, persuaded many Presbyterians, Baptists, Congregationalists, and others to join them. Similarly, American Christians, deeply hurt by racism in 1975, pull those they can influence out of segregated churches into integrated ones. But this is exactly as it should be. Christians should be free to persuade and counter persuade.

Well-fed sheep cannot be stolen. Convinced Christians stay in their own churches. They steadily refuse to join other congregations. Indeed, so true is this, and so basic to a right understanding of the whole thorny issue, that with only a slight degree of exaggeration, one may say of sheep that 'if they can be stolen, it is not sheep stealing.' Finding sheep running wild in the streets, or hungry on the mountain side and bringing them back to the fold is not sheep stealing. It is engaging in Christ's work of finding and folding the lost.

In Allahabad, India about four miles from the city center, a suburb had developed at Naini. In it lived fourteen people who belonged to the downtown Church North India. They almost never went to church or saw their pastor. Then in Naini, the Evangelical Church of India (a small denomination) started two new congregations which took in these fourteen and others. The downtown church angrily charged sheep stealing. To which the pastor of the Evangelical Church serenely replied, "Splendid! You go on sleeping and we'll go on stealing."

I would not be understood as condoning a mean-spirited raiding of other congregations. It is sin to disturb the faith of Christians, who are happily a part of another church, unless one gives them something more biblical. To get Christians to change affiliation, without any deeper understanding of the Lord or any more obedient relation to Him, is to be condemned. Furthermore, charges of sheep stealing are usually exaggerated.

Dr. Robert Schuller writes that, while he condemns divisive competitive practices, he works "as if our church were the only church in a population of a half million, and we are responsible for the salvation of all the people there." No wonder his church has grown enormously.

During the past fifty years, most pastors in North America have leaned over backward to avoid the charge of "sheep stealing." Partly as a result of this, about a hundred million Americans are nominal, marginal, or slightly lapsed Christians. What is now demanded is that every church seek to be a better church—to have more biblical teaching, warmer fellowship, more Christian love, more concern for social justice, and more effective evangelism of the lost. When a prospect says, "I belong to another church," he ought to be asked in as kindly a way as possible, "Are you a **practicing** Christian?" If the answer to these questions are not satisfactory, he (a sheep running wild on the range) ought to be found and folded, fed and transformed.

If this be sheep stealing, let us steal boldly!

Organizing Laity for Outreach

BY DR. KENNETH VAN WYK

A vital ingredient of church growth is the "people-power" required to implement it. The narrative of Christ's Church through Scripture and history is eloquent witness to the fact that God uses His people to grow His church. The Great Commission clearly states that Christ's disciples are relied upon to propagate the faith. This does not refer to a few highly gifted clergymen; it refers to the laity of the church. The growth of the church is not a solo operation; it is a united effort of the Body—God's people—working in concert and obedience to the Head—Jesus Christ. Van Wyk considers the foundation essential to any organizing of lay leaders for growth and outreach, in this first of two articles.

It is natural for ambitious church leaders to want instant lay leadership for church growth. And it is tempting to go directly to the mimeograph machine and duplicate a program booklet outlining "A Training Program for the Laity."

Dr. Kenneth Van Wyk is Minister of Education at Garden Grove Community Church, Garden Grove, California.

Experience indicates, however, that patience must be exercised. Lay leadership does not come overnight. It is developed over a long period of time. Furthermore, it must be built upon the foundation of an adequate theology. It is sad but true that the church has had more than its quota of program failures. Some have failed due to inadequate theological foundation; others have failed because of administrative deficiency. A program of training lay leadership will be just one more failure unless adequate preparation and groundwork is laid. The proper starting point is not program ideas, but rather the biblical foundation undergirding the program. Hendrik Kraemer states that all lay activity "...will ultimately fail if it has no lasting and serious theological foundation. It will appear in the future mere temporary effervescence or a passing erruption of activism, without real backbone, if it is not undergirded by a well-thought-out theology of the laity on a biblical basis, which becomes a natural and inalienable part of that new-common understanding of the church..."[1]

The following six biblical concepts are foundation stones on which the training of laity for church growth is built.

1. THE CHURCH—ONE CLASS OF PEOPLE

The proper starting point in lay mobilization is a biblical understanding of the members who comprise the church. Today they are commonly called the laity. This term goes back to the Greek word "laikos." It designates those who belong to the "laos" or the chosen people of God. Thus, all who profess faith in Jesus Christ as Lord, men and women, are God's chosen "laos." They have been called out of the mass of mankind and have given allegiance to Him.[2]

Influenced by the Graeco-Roman political environment, the church began to divide the people into two classes. The "kleros" (the word from which the term "clergy" stems) were those who possessed wisdom, were trained, and had power to act. The "laos" (the word from which the term "laity" stems) were those who were untrained and who were expected to submit to direction.

This ecclesiastical development of dividing the church into two classes of adults—clergy and laity—is a departure from the biblical concept of the whole church as "laos." In the New Testament the word "kleros," when used in regard to the new community in Christ, is always meant as the body of men and women who share in God's gift of redemption and glory, which is their inheritance, because they are incorporated in the Son. There is no shimmer of an idea of a definite body, called "Clergy."[3] Thus, the two words "kleros" (clergy) and "laos" (laity) refer to the same people in the New Testament.

The Reformation in the sixteenth century brought promise of correcting the corrupted concept of clergy and laity that had grown up in the church. In principle the distinction between clergy and laity was abolished, and the priesthood of all believers was proclaimed. The Reformers reaffirmed the New Testament teaching that all are priests called by God to perform His ministry in the world. "But you are a chosen race, a royal priesthood, a holy nation, God's own people, that you may declare the wonderful deeds of him who called you out of darkness into his marvelous light" (I Peter 2:9). However, in the stress and heat of the Reformation, this principle was never fully brought into practice. The whole concept of ministry was left ambiguous. The laity remained largely as objects of ministry instead of being ministers in their own right.[4]

2. CLERGY AND LAITY—A COMMON MINISTRY

It appears that the church will not soon divest itself of the old concepts traditionally held. However, even though the terms "clergy" and "laity" are still used with some of the old connotations, a new understanding of their roles is emerging. Out of the conventional view of the pastor as the person whom the congregation hires to perform the work of ministry, the biblical concept is now emerging which sees the pastor and people together as responsible for the work of ministry. Together they make up the church, the Body of Christ, and together they carry out the ministry of Christ given to the Body. There is a difference of function, but each ministry is a service for Christ and, as such, of equal status.

3. LAITY AS MINISTERS

A very important fact surfaces in this larger concept of the role of the laity. It is, simply, that the laity must come into a new sense of identity. Through the process of re-education, they must come to see who they really are in God's eyes. The words of the biblical writer seem oddly appropriate to the emerging identity of the laity, "Once you were no people, but now you are God's people..." With the loss of their role identity, their rightful position is only belatedly being recognized. It must be remembered that no lay training program will function unless the laity know who they are and what their role is. To set up a program without first building the concept of lay ministry in the congregation is a significant procedural error.

4. PASTORS AND TEACHERS AS TRAINERS

There is a second very important implication on the new role of the laity. If the work of ministry is committed to the adult believers of the church, as the New Testament teaches, who is responsible for training these adults for their task? This is where the original role of the pastor comes into focus. The New Testament indicates the task of the pastors and teachers of the church: "And his gifts were that some should be... pastors and teachers, for the equipment of the saints, for the work of ministry, for building up the body of Christ..." (Eph. 4:11,12). B.F. Westcott explains this significant verse as follows: "However foreign the idea of the spiritual ministry of all 'the saints' is to our mode of thinking, it was crucial to the life of the apostolic Church. The responsible officers of the congregation work through others, and find no rest till everyone fulfills his function... The work of the ministry is directed to the preparation of the saints—the whole body of the faithful—for the twofold work which in due measure belongs to all Christians, a personal work and a social work. Every believer is charged with the duty of personal service to his fellow-believers and to his fellowmen, and has some part in building up the fabric of the Christian Society."[5]

Thus, we see that the "laos," to whom the ministry of the church is committed, is made up of pastors who do the training and the laity who carry out the ministry. This clearly is a reversal of the traditionally accepted roles. Therefore, a re-education process is necessary so that the pastor can wholeheartedly accept this new role. This is very important, because the success of the lay training program depends upon the pastor's willingness to train the lay ministers of the congregation. It is equally important that the pastor give significant areas of ministry to the trained lay ministers so that they can function in their new role. The laity will be motivated only to the extent that significant areas of ministry are given to their charge. The pastor who is emotionally secure and biblically aware will be the pastor most facilitative to a lay ministers' training program. The dynamic needed to make a training program effective in the local church is the mutual understanding and enthusiastic acceptance of the redefined roles of laity and pastor.

5. CHRIST'S MODEL FOR MINISTRY

Should either pastor or layperson begin to wonder about the steadiness of the biblical foundation upon which this new role of ministry rests, the example of Jesus Christ as Head of the Church should suffice to restore confidence. A careful reading of the Gospels reveals an important strategy of Christ's short three-year ministry. He devoted Himself to the training of a small group of laymen. He might have reasoned that He did not have time to give to this small group of disciples when the multitudes could have had his full time and energies. Yet, the Gospels indicate that Jesus gave as much time training the twelve as He gave to the masses. When the time came for His departure, Jesus commissioned His trainees: "Go therefore and make disciples of all nations..." The history of the early Christian Church is eloquent witness to the wisdom of Christ's role as trainer of the twelve and the disciples' role as those who minister.

The pastor cannot teach all the people of the church in the same manner as Christ taught the twelve. He will need help from other teachers in this task. However, it is wise for the pastor to disciple a small group of lay people who give of themselves to an in-depth training course. In this way, a group of well-trained laity will become the "leaven" in the congregation which builds up grass roots enthusiasm for the expanding role of the lay ministers. These trained lay people become trainers of others in the congregation.

6. THE CHURCH AS MISSION

Another key element in the biblical foundation for training lay leadership is the mission of the church. It is clear from verses such as Matt. 28:19, John 17:18, Acts 1:8 and I Peter 2:9 that Christ's will for His Church is to "...go make disciples of all nations..."; for "...I have sent them into the world..."; and "...to the ends of the earth."; "...that you may declare the wonderful deeds of him who called you out of darkness into his marvelous light." These passages are representative of the over-arching theme of Scripture that God calls His people to give themselves in loving ministry to His lost sheep. The life of Christ is the pattern for all His followers. "For the Son of man also came not to be served but to serve, and to give his life a ransom for many" (Mk. 10:45).

A study of the history of the people of God in the Old and New Testament reveals an interesting fact: the well-being of the believing community was directly proportional to their obedience to God's mission for them. When the people of God have a sense of mission (some term it *a sense of destiny*) things go well and the church is strong and healthy. When the church becomes introverted and loses its desire to minister in Christ's name to those who are in need, problems set in.

This biblical principle has significant implications for the lay training program. It emphatically indicates that the heartbeat for the program in the local church must be *training for mission*. The poison of most adult education programs has been their basic introversion. A look at the goals of adult Christian education in the major denominations reveals that the training for mission is not in sharp focus.[6] Church growth studies verify that churches that limit their training energies to "in-house" needs are churches without a growth record.[7] When the church expends itself for the sake of others, it becomes healthy and grows. When the people of a church catch the vision of being a part of the answer to the hurts and needs of the world around them, they gain incentive for participating in a training program designed to equip them for this purpose. Jesus said "...whoever loses his life for my sake will find it" (Matt. 16:25). When Christ's followers lose themselves in something far bigger than themselves, namely Christ's work, they find themselves. This is an amazing paradox. Yet, it is absolutely true as the history of the church so amply tells us. By the same token, the lay training program must never be an end in itself. It is a means to an end. *That end is the mission of the church.* Lay training, then, must be designed to equip God's people for the ministry or mission to which He has called them.

FOOTNOTES

1. Kraemer, Hendrik. *A Theology of the Laity.* Philadelphia: Westminster Press, 1958, p. 13.
2. Stott, John R.W. *One People.* Downers Grove, Illinois: Inter Varsity Press, 1968.
3. Kraemer, Hendrik. *A Theology of the Laity.* Philadelphia: Westminster Press, 1958, p. 52.
4. Robinson, William. "Completing the Reformation: The Doctrine of the Priesthood of All Believers," The College of the Bible Quarterly, July 1955, Vol. XXXII, No. 3, p. 11 ff.
5. Westcott, B.F. *Epistle to the Ephesians.* Grand Rapids, Michigan: Erdmans, 1952, p. 62.
6. Ziegler, Earl F. *Christian Education of Adults,* Philadelphia: Westminster Press, 1958, p. 46 ff.
7. McGavran, Donald A. and Arn, Win. *How to Grow a Church,* Glendale, California: Gospel Light Publications, 1973, p. 89 ff.

A Workable Model for Training the Laity BY KENNETH VAN WYK

Important as the biblical foundation is for building an adequate lay training program, it alone is not sufficient. The biblical principles must be put into practice. All is for naught if the local church is not able to translate the concepts into an actual working program. There is a scarcity of workable models in the field for the local church to pattern. Religious groups such as the Mormons and the Jehovah's Witnesses have outdone the mainline Protestant Church in their ability to effectively train their people for ministry. It is the purpose of this article to propose a working model for the local church, based on my own experience and the experience of others. It involves four major steps.

1. BUILD MOMENTUM FOR LAY INVOLVEMENT IN THE MISSION OF THE CHURCH

The starting point in our own church experiment was an adult Bible study program called the *Bethel Series*.[1] This program provided an important impetus for the lay movement in the congregation. It provided a growing awareness that God calls His people to greatness. He pours His blessing into their lives, calls them to be a blessing to others, and promises that through their lives people of all nations will be blessed (Gen. 12:1-3). This basic biblical theme is traced through a study of the history of God's people from Abraham through the early Christian Church. The result is that many adults catch the vision of greatness to which God has called them. They develop a desire to be a part of God's redemptive movement. Along with this impetus from a study program, the pulpit is of key significance in giving the laity a vision for becoming involved in the church's mission. The enthusiasm of the pastor for this new direction has tremendous power in motivating the laity. Building a sense of mission in the lives of the laity is the all important aspect of training laity for church growth. It's the heartbeat and motivation for mission. To fail here is fatal!

2. DEVELOP THE LAY-MINISTER IDENTITY

The pastor is a strategic person for building the self-concept of the people of the congregation. When people hear the pastor say that they are real players on the Christian team and that the pastor is the coach, a new sense of identity begins to form. When this is sincerely believed and the words are translated into actions, the laity move forward to accept the challenge.

An education program, in concert with the pulpit, is needed to build the lay-minister identity. Through a study of the biblical narrative the lay person begins to see that the backbone of God's redemptive program through history is people who, like themselves, become available to be God's blessing to others. Many lay people in the church today have an inferiority complex. They fail to see that they are God's ministers and that great things can be accomplished through them. A properly focused study builds the believers' self-image and creates within them the identity as God's agents of redemption. This dynamic is essential to the transition of the laity from a spectator role to the role of active participant in the life and mission of the church.

3. UTILIZE CHRIST'S PATTERN OF DISCIPLING

Christ believed in the principle that a small group of well-trained disciples could permeate a larger group in much the same way that a little yeast in the dough leavens the whole loaf (Luke 13:21). Jesus not only taught this principle, He also put it into practice in the training of the twelve. It was through the investment of Himself in an intimate, instructive, and purposeful relationship that Jesus equipped the twelve. Through the course of a few years, He trained them by indelibly stamping their lives with a model of ministry they could not forget.

This pattern is important for the church today in developing an authentic lay ministry. Our Minister of Education trains clusters of lay men and women who give themselves to a discipline of weekly study and interaction. The Bethel Series teacher training program is used. To date, four groups of twenty lay people have taken this two-year Bible survey training program. There are homework assignments requiring eight to ten hours of preparation per week. After two years together with the pastor, these trained lay people agree to accept a two-year work assignment for which they have been prepared. The influence of these people is pervasive. Their enthusiasm and growth dimension becomes a positive incentive for lay ministry in the life of the entire congregation. These trained lay people become trainers of other lay persons in the church.

4. DEVELOP A LAY-MINISTERS TRAINING CENTER

As the lay-consciousness develops, the church is ready to set up its own lay-ministers training center. Again it must be emphasized that the dynamics of lay ministry must be inculcated in the life of the congregation *before* a training center can be effective.

The church must begin by determining the needed areas of ministry, both in the life of the church and in the community. For example, we determined that one of the areas of need was to train lay people as evangelists to share Christ with the unchurched. In addition, it was clear that a large number of lay people would need to be trained to carry out the teaching ministry for all ages in the Christian education program. Because the total membership of the congregation is divided into family units according to geographic location, lay leaders needed to be trained to carry out pastoral care in these small membership clusters—scattered throughout the county. A telephone counseling ministry was started to help the hurting members of our community who call in with crises and problem situations. These lay telephone counselors needed specialized training to man the telephones. It was determined that 35,000 out of the 1,646,000 people in our county were functionally illiterate. A special training program for the lay tutors, using the Laubach Each-One-Teach-One method, was initiated so that the church could respond to this need. These are illustrations of the answers our church has given to the question, "What is Christ asking us, as a church, to do in response to His call of service?"

Each church must individually determine what the answers are to that all-important question. A church that does not determine its mission in the light of Scripture and in view of the needs of its community is not likely to grow. Nor will a lay training center be effective in a church that does not have its essential mission and purpose in sharp focus. It is the mission-minded church that motivates lay people to be on the march for Christ. And it is lay people who catch the vision of the forward movement of the church that are motivated to get involved in the work of Christ. These are the people who respond to training opportunities because they see it as a step toward the fulfillment of Christ's call.

The next step was to ascertain the kind of training needed to equip the lay-ministers to accomplish the predetermined objectives. Our Lay-Ministers Training Center uses the pattern of a seven-week term offered in the fall, winter and spring as a midweek training program. Courses are offered in the areas of the Bible, the Church, the Christian Life, and Ministry. Bible courses include a study of individual books of the Bible, a study of the life of Christ, and a course in beginning Bible study for those who need an introductory study.

Courses in the area of the Church are church history, Christian doctrine, and a study of other faiths. Topics such as Christian ethics, marriage and the family, finances, interpersonal relationships, prayer, discovery and use of spiritual gifts are samples of courses in the Christian Life area. Ministry courses are the practical courses that provide the specific "how-to" for each area where the laity are involved in service for Christ.

The classes meet for one hour in seven-week terms and require homework, usually on the basis of two hours per class period. In most instances textbooks are used. As the lay person progresses in his prescribed course of study, he attains recognized levels of achievement. Course instructors are, for the most part, secured from the membership and staff of the congregation. Credit is given for training on the job as well as training received in the classroom. After an accumulation of 224 credit hours, which ordinarily takes about five years, the participants are recognized in the congregation as Credentialed Lay Ministers. They become a well-trained cadre of leaders in the life of the church, fulfilling leadership assignments commensurate with their skills and training.

The training program need not be elaborate; it only needs to be functional. It should be tailor-made to the needs and goals of the individual congregation. It is tempting for small congregations to feel that they are not able to have their own training programs, but something is lost when the laity are trained outside the local church. The church functions best when it helps its own members to discover their identity and role in the mission of their own local church. Each member has a gift of service that needs to be activated toward the proper functioning of the church body (I Cor. 12; Rom. 12; Eph. 4; I Peter 4). The biblical analogy of the church to the organism of the human body as taught in Scripture carries the implication that the church is to help its members identify their gifts and train them in their proper use.[2] In this way, the body is able to function and carry out its divinely assigned mission.

The Lay-Ministers Training Center is like a locally based theological seminary designed to train the laity. The Center follows a modified academic model. Years of experience from the education community indicate that the academic model does not guarantee automatic success. It is possible for a person to do all the course work and remain ill equipped to serve. What are the safeguards against this kind of educational ineffectiveness?

One of the greatest antidotes to aimless and unproductive course work is the motivation and sense of purpose of the trainee. Participants who progress in the training program are people who are deeply involved in some phase of Christ's mission. They, like Abraham of old, have heard the Lord saying to them, "...I will bless you...so that you will be a blessing..." (Gen. 12:1-3). The training courses are the means of equipping them so that they can more effectively be a blessing to others. This motivation for training is absolutely crucial, because it adds the dimension of relevancy and meaning necessary to make education effective and dynamic.

A second equally important safeguard is the discipling concept. In the discipling process the leader is able to focus his attention on small clusters of trainees. Through an affirming, supportive, facilitative role the trainer helps the lay person to develop and grow as a person in the performance of his ministry. This enabling role of the trainer is crucial to the success of lay training. As a coach-player he can give time and personalized attention to the trainees. The trained leader who has charge over a specific area of service needs to provide a pattern to be imitated in ministry. This trainer teaches the ministry courses for his specific area of service in the Training Center and becomes the discipler of the lay people involved in his area. The leader is the one to whom the workers are accountable and is their enabler in ministry.

A concluding word needs to be added to define what is meant by the word "growth." It must be acknowledged that some churches are in communities where numerical growth is not likely to be sizeable. But every church is surrounded with needs! Christ wants His people to fill these needs for His sake. Christ identified Himself with human need. He expended Himself in filling these needs. He taught the Church to follow His example, "...as you did it to one of the least of these my brethren, you did it to me" (Matt. 25:40).

There are churches that are motivating and training their people to be involved redemptively in the human hurts around them. People are being helped and lives are being changed. The church is obedient to Christ when it is fulfilling His mission in their community.

Growth essentially is determined by a church's obedience to Christ's mission as set forth in Scripture. It is for this high calling that the church trains her laity. The great need of our time is that the church take this calling seriously.

FOOTNOTES

1. *The Bethel Series.* Adult Christian Education Foundation, 313 Price Place, Box 5305, Madison, Wisconsin 53705.
2. Yohn, Rick. *Discover Your Spiritual Gift and Use It.* Wheaton, Illinois: Tyndale House Publishers, 1974.

Some Practical Ways to Begin BY GEORGE HUNTER

The church growth definition of "evangelism" is: "Proclaiming Jesus Christ as God and Savior and persuading people to become His disciples and responsible members of His Church." This definition, and subsequent task of the church in fulfilling Christ's Great Commission, has been broken down into the more "bite-size" pieces of A) Preparation, B) Presence, C) Proclamation, D) Persuasion, and E)

"EFFECTIVE EVANGELISM"

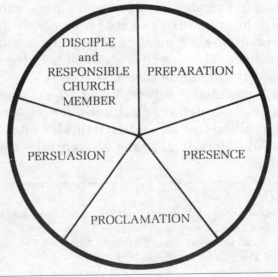

Dr. Hunter is Secretary for Evangelism, United Methodist Board of Discipleship.

Responsible Church Membership.[1] Below are some tools for moving from the "theoretical" to the "practical" in each of these critical areas:

A. PREPARATION

What football team could expect success in playing an entire game without a huddle? Or what contractor could expect a substantial building without a blueprint? What church can expect significant growth without an adequate degree of preparation? It's all a matter of planning.

1. Community Survey. Begin with "Church Growth Eyes" and a search for "prospects." Prospects can be discovered through an extensive survey of your "ministry area" (that area within a reasonable driving distance of the church). This telephone and door-to-door surveying will give many laymen an experience that will excite them with the new possibilities of outreach for their church. But the central purpose is to index the names and addresses of unchurched people (including "nominal" members not currently involved in any community of faith), people who have a "preference" for the denomination, and people who seem to be receptive.

2. Begin Record Keeping. These index cards contain the data of prospective Christians and should be filed, with one person in charge. Because these cards represent people, the church should never risk losing a card. In time, you may want to expand to two files—one based on the receptivity of persons, and one based on geography—to enable the greatest visiting for the least traveling.

3. Begin Training. Laymen will rightly feel the need for training and will be reluctant to become actively involved without it. The training and preparation ought to include: (a) biblical foundation that grounds church growth in the very purpose and will of God, (b) principles of effective church growth, (c) methods that can be successfully employed by your church, (d) practice, which would include both role-playing and on-the-job training.

4. Establish Support Groups. Laymen will need the support and encouragement of each other if they are to be consistent and grow in outreach. The understanding, learning, support, and empowerment that each person will receive from this koinonia is indispensable to the church's long-term ministry, and provides a continuing sense of unity in purpose.

5. Pray for Empowerment. The Holy Spirit goes before us, and we follow. There is much that can be known about strategies and methods of communicating the Gospel, but whenever communication and response takes place, it is *His work* through our methods. We must always be more dependent on Christ's enabling Spirit than we are on our best strategies and methods.

B. PRESENCE

Evangelistic strategy begins by achieving a *presence* with those we desire to attract to the Faith. The achievement of Presence is intrinsically worthwhile. In these "presence ministries," it is not necessary that one always (or even usually) verbalize the Gospel. The Christian has not "failed" if he has not mentioned Christ's name. The essential purpose of these ministries is to know people, to be known by them, to identify with them, and to demonstrate a caring interest in them. These ministries are vital.

1. Telephone Ministries. Some people have real gifts (and experience) for communicating over the telephone. A variety of ministries can be performed, from calls to people who have visited the church, to birthday and other "special event" calls, to crisis telephone ministries. Shut-in persons can frequently minister by telephone, especially to each other.

2. Direct Mail Advertising. Develop a professional, communicative piece that speaks to the needs of the people in your ministry area and explains how the church can help. With an attractive cover letter, this mailing will put the church's presence in front of every potential new member. Put considerable thought and planning into this, however, or it could be a very loud proclamation that "the church down the street" doesn't know heads from tails.

3. Friendly Visits. These visits go beyond church-affiliation surveying in that the purpose is to visit, to get to know, to establish credibility, trust, and acquaintanceship, to discover needs to which the church can minister. Visiting and getting to know neighbors is an enjoyable exercise.

4. Providing Service. Every church has (or should begin) ministries that meet human needs in their ministry area. Day care centers, mothers-day-out programs, "meals-on-wheels," Parent Effectiveness Training, Big Brothers, counseling services, special groups (scouts, senior citizens, etc.) are some random examples. The role of presence evangelism here might be to inform people of these services and invite those who need them to participate. Or the offer might be more unstructured, as in the case of the *Oak Lane Presbyterian Church* in Philadelphia which asks people, "How can we be of help to you?"

5. Visiting Visitors. People who visit the church are statistically among the most receptive people in your ministry area. They should be telephoned that afternoon and visited that week. The purpose of these visits is to express interest in people, to get to know them and be known by them, to inquire regarding their beliefs, relation to Christ, and perhaps for church membership. A "hard sell" to casual church visitors would be counterproductive. You very well may, in this ministry, engage in "church referral." As you find out what the people are "looking for," if in your judgment another church could better meet their need—your greatest service might be in referring them to *that* church!

6. Calling Inactive Members. In certain cases, inactive members are also a very responsive population. But their renewal in the Body of Christ requires the initiative of active church members. It is even worthwhile to reach out to those whom we cannot reactivate—for the feedback they can give us. If we learn how we failed them, that should prevent us from failing the same way again.

C. PROCLAMATION

It is crucial that we share the Gospel with all persons who "have ears to hear," because "faith comes by hearing the word of God." How is this to be done by today's laypeople? The strategy a church develops must be unique to every congregation. The forms our witness takes must be considered to maximize effectiveness. To sling texts and tracts at people or regurgitate slogans and memorized lines will not usually be effective. Nor will blind importation of a method that worked somewhere else be sufficient. Our forms of witness must be creative and incarnational to which secular people can respond.

1. Organize and Host Neighborhood Groups in which non-Christians can explore the Christian faith. Research is finding that many persons will accept an invitation to come to a home meeting who would not think of attending a Sunday service. Such groups will be, for many people, the threshold into the local church. The agenda must be the basics of the Christian Gospel, expressed in quite secular language, correlating the message with the felt needs and motives of the people—and all within a setting of warm, supportive, affirming fellowship.

2. Christian Literature is an often overlooked medium of proclaiming the Gospel to non-Christians. We overlook it, perhaps, because most people are "turned off" by tracts or because people may not read a lot of books. But the popularity in this generation of such books as *Love Story* and *Jonathan Livingston Seagull* teach us that people in great numbers will read something interesting that can be completed in an evening. *TIDINGS* (the evangelism publishing arm of the United Methodist Church) reports very great success in the sales of its first three small books in the "Pass-it-On" series: *How To Find God,* by Keith Miller; *Who Is Jesus Christ?* by William Barclay; and *What Is the Meaning of Life?* by Alan Walker.

3. Deploy Teams for Ministry to Persons in Transitions. There is abundant evidence that people in transition are more receptive than people in stability. This principle applies to many transitions, and not merely the several that are usually thought of as "crises." The stock transitions which most people experience, during (and shortly after) which they are likely more receptive, include: adolescence, going to college or armed services, first job, getting married, first child, last child leaves home, menopause, male menopause, retirement. Stock transitions that many people experience, in addition, include: moving, suffering, loss of loved one, separation, divorce, getting fired, job advancement. During and shortly after such changes in one's situation or social role, people tend to be fairly receptive to a change in life style.

A church that took this fact with strategic seriousness would prepare cadres of its members for relevant ministry and witness to such transitional persons. They would be chosen by special gifts, interest, expertise, or background —as, for instance, sending out to persons experiencing divorce a team of two or three Christians who had divorce in their background and discovered the resources of Grace and Koinonia for this painful transition.

The church's strategy for persons in transition should be based on two elements: (1) have a team of Christians for each transition, i.e., if you identify ten transitions to which you can minister—have ten teams; (2) sensitize, by special effort, the entire congregation to act as a referral system. For instance, if any member hears of someone who was fired, or is divorcing, or just retired, etc., that member telephones the church secretary, who takes the information and relays it to the appropriate ministry team in the church.

4. Inviting People to Join in Service is a neglected strategy in most churches, but has great potential. Many persons have needs (self-esteem, self-realization, making one's life count, etc.) which can be met as a by-product of giving themselves to some cause or service of the church's mission. If a church is doing worthwhile things for people, its most effective evangelical appeal to many bright, strong, achievement-oriented persons will be to offer the opportunity for significant service through the church. Through such experiences, many of these people will "taste the Kingdom of God," and this experience will be self-authenticating. Christians, while participating with not-yet-Christians in Christian service, will relate to them.

5. Door-to-Door Witnessing in Homes in a target area is a genre which, although conventional, should not be overlooked. Although it may not be the most strategic way of developing your witnesses, it is a fool-proof method of assuring that no person in your ministry area is neglected, and is one way of discovering receptive people. Naturally, *what* you say to people, and *how*, and *where* are crucial variables in this ministry. We must take seriously our Lord's strong metaphor—"Do not cast your pearls before swine," i.e., we are not constrained to proclaim the Gospel to *all* persons as we find them now. For the first visit, only a ministry of presence and listening may be possible. We may justly ask permission to share something of our faith. Where people are in fact receptive, or at least open, we may indeed share a great deal. What we say should follow a careful listening to and understanding of this person, and should be correlated to what we have perceived of the person's unique problems and needs.

6. Visit the Town Agnostics and the "Tough Situations." We are not called to abandon any people or setting. Some of our more articulate and inwardly strong Christians might visit bars, jails, city hall, or whatever setting and people are indifferent or hostile to Christ and the Church. The direct "returns" from such ministry will be fairly low, but it will strengthen witnesses engaged in this apologetic ministry, and will establish the public image of the church as a community that both cares and dares.

D. PERSUASION

Everything we have done in the preparation, presence, and proclamation ministries is for the sake of making disciples, i.e., persuading people to become followers to Jesus and responsible members of His Body. Nothing that we have done prior to this was an end in itself—although it may have been intrinsically worth doing. God calls to people through Jesus Christ that they might turn to Him, open their beings to Him, obey Him, and so find life.

Donald McGavran, in the film *Reach Out and Grow*, comments, "Persuasion is a part of life. We constantly persuade people. I persuade you, you persuade me. I suggest to a friend that he buy a new razor because it gives a wonderful shave. We persuade people to play a game of tennis, or read a book, or buy some new product. Persuasion is just an essential part of life. And evangelism simply extends that normal, beautiful activity into the spiritual realm."

The ministry of persuasion requires that we sometimes share the Gospel and appeal for *response*. That "sometimes" is God's *kairos* moment when a person is perceived as being receptive or when an evangelical conversation naturally leads this far. Some people have the spiritual gifts to enable others not only toward, but into an initial Christian experience. All witnesses should extend the option as they discover that possibility in conversations, but your gifted lay "discipling specialists" should especially be sent to persons who are thought to be on the threshold of a decision to commit their life to Christ.

E. DISCIPLE and RESPONSIBLE CHURCH MEMBER

Bishop J. Wascom Pickett demonstrated four decades ago that what we do with people in the weeks immediately after they make a decision for Christ is crucial. Indeed, his study of 3,947 converts concluded that their "post-baptismal training" was more influential in whether they remained and grew in the Christian community, than even the motives from which they were originally attracted to Christianity. McGavran and Arn, in their latest book, *Ten Steps for Church Growth*, state, "A decision is often the first step; however, we deceive ourselves if we believe that a person who has made a decision for Christ, who has prayed, 'I accept Jesus Christ into my life,' has truly become a disciple. A 'decision' suggests a brief moment in time. A 'disciple' suggests a life-long task."

Of course, the convert's solid entry into the church is not merely a cognitive entry, but also a relational entry. The church must move intentionally to create a relational support system that will create in the convert a sense of being known in, and belonging to, the people of God. Two strategies are especially promising.

1. One strategy is a *sponsors* program. The convert should be assigned a sponsor (or in the case of a joining couple, a sponsoring couple). A sponsor ought to represent the same homogeneous population as the convert. The sponsor will introduce the new member to people and groups, and to opportunities in the church. The sponsor will be available to the new member, will consult with him for the first year of the new member's life in the congregation. The original "matchup" between sponsor and convert is not etched in granite. If it turns out they are "mismatched," the convert should be assigned another sponsor. Fairly recent converts (one to four years) frequently make excellent sponsors, so look among your maturing converts for promising sponsors of new converts.

2. Another basic strategy for relational support is your church's *group system.* Every convert ought to become quickly involved in the life of some group connected with the church, whether a Sunday School class, a prayer group, a choir, or an age group. Group involvement should be *required* for the convert (as for all members), because most Christians cannot remain vital or grow in the Life except as that Life is propagated through Christian Koinonia.

3. Of course, the new convert's entry into Christian life and community is not only cognitive and relational, but also behavioral. This means two additional requirements. One is corporate worship, in which the convert rehearses and reinforces his new identity within the people of God The other requirement is service. Every convert is called to engage in whatever ministry(s) of the church is/are appropriate to the "gifts" of the individual. Frequently the new convert's most effective point of service is back on the battlefield. A new Christian's friends and associates are mostly non-Christian, and his new-found enthusiasm should be directed toward this receptive area.

These ideas will hopefully be a source of mental and spiritual stimulation. There are myriad techniques to effective evangelism that churches have found successful for their particular situations. But remember the 5-step strategy. Without that overriding structure, our churches will be less than effective stewards of Christ's ultimate purpose and desire for His Church.

FOOTNOTE

1. Institute for American Church Growth; Basic Seminar.

A Church Growth Look at...

Here's Life America BY DR. WIN ARN

"Unprecedented Spiritual Awakening Sweeping the Country," shout the lines of the paper published by Campus Crusade to promote "Here's Life America." "Greatest Spiritual Harvest in the History of the Church," says Bill Bright, President of Crusade, "100 times yes, 1000 times greater than anything I have ever seen or read about in the almost 2000-year-old history of the Church." "I believe that one can truthfully say that here in the United States the Great Commission will be fulfilled by the end of this year."

Quite impressive! And very encouraging...if it is true. And let's hope it is. But let's also take a closer look at "Here's Life America"...a look through Church Growth Eyes.

First, what is "Here's Life America"? It is a program sponsored by Campus Crusade aimed at saturating metropolitan areas and smaller communities with the message of Christ through a multi-media campaign including billboards, bumperstickers, newspaper ads, radio, and television. Under the slogan "I found it," churches and laymen are recruited to answer telephone calls, deliver

Dr. Win Arn is President of the Institute for American Church Growth, Pasadena, California.

booklets, contact homes by telephone to explain the "four spiritual laws," and eventually seek a commitment to repeat a prayer to accept Christ. The goal of the program is to saturate the country, and eventually the world, with this approach.

What are "Church Growth Eyes"? The term refers to a developed characteristic of individuals and churches who have achieved a sensitivity to seeing possibilities, based on fact gathering and analysis, and who apply effective appropriate strategies to reap maximum results for Christ and the Church.

Characteristics of people with Church Growth Eyes:

1. They endeavor to see the world from God's perspective: people outside of Jesus Christ are really lost, and God urgently wants them found.

2. They endeavor to examine and research why some Christian works are fruitful while others are impotent... why some results last and others do not.

3. They endeavor to devise bold plans and strategies, under the guidance of the Holy Spirit, which produce actual, factual growth of the Church...growth which brings people into churches as disciples and responsible members...growth which is measurable in one year and five years...growth which reproduces itself in new disciples.

When a person with Church Growth Eyes sees fellow Christians determined to be obedient to the Great Commission, they are seen as "comrades in arms."

But what does it mean to be obedient to the Great Commission? The goal of the Great Commission, from a Church Growth perspective, is the establishment of a cell (church) of committed Christians in every community, every neighborhood, every class and condition of people, where everyone can hear and see demonstrated the Gospel from his own intimates, in his own tongue, and has a reasonable opportunity to become a disciple of Jesus Christ.

With this Great Commission objective, let us take a closer look at "Here's Life America."

1. Question: IS THE GOAL OF "HERE'S LIFE" ADEQUATE?

A major goal of "Here's Life America" is decisions for Christ. Success is measured, as in most mass evangelistic endeavors, by the number who make a verbal commitment. The higher that number, the more successful the method.

Here's a quote from the "Here's Life America" promotional piece in front of me. *"This man was one of more than 1700 recorded decisions..."* The emphasis is on recorded decisions. A similar indication is found in *Christianity Today* (September 24, 1976) where Bill Bright says, "One of our staff members trained several volunteers, who then interviewed 7400 people on the telephone. 47% of those not already Christian prayed with the caller, and received Christ." The questioner then asked, "Do you think they were really born again?" Bright responded, "I don't know. I would not know if they came to the altar of a church and wept for an hour..."

While it is true that only God knows the heart, as stewards of the grace of God, can we be satisfied that our work is finished when a person answers with an initial "yes" to a series of questions and repeats the lines of a prayer? A person with Church Growth Eyes could not be satisfied with only a verbal commitment. He would be concerned with the nature and establishment of those decisions. Were they indeed genuine? Are they being discipled? Are they part of a community of believers—the Church? It is not enough to simply wish hard that they become established in a church...for wishing does not make it so. Effective evangelism demands that built into the decision-making process is *incorporation* into the Body of Christ.

The Edmonton Campus Crusade director gave me their definition of evangelism: "Taking the initiative to share Christ in the power of the Holy Spirit and leaving the results up to God." From a Church Growth viewpoint, this definition is inadequate. Why not a definition which includes "taking the initiative to share Christ in the power of the Holy Spirit...making disciples in the power of the Holy Spirit...incorporating into the Body of Christ in the power of the Holy Spirit...?"

Is a goal for "decisions" adequate? John F. Alexander (*"Evangelism in Breadth and Depth," The Other Side*) writes: "What God wants is not simply an oral confession: He wants something deeper...a completely transformed life...if we are to fulfill the Great Commission, we must present the Gospel not as easy-believism, but as life-transforming discipleship..."

Is this not the biblical concept? I think so. While getting decisions has been part of the evangelistic "modus operandi" since the days of the "sawdust trail," it is not a biblical concept! The word "decision" is never found in Scripture. The word "disciple" appears over 260 times.

Unquestionably, the biblical concept is to make disciples. The Church Growth conviction of evangelism captures that intent when it defines evangelism as "Proclaiming Jesus Christ as God and Savior, persuading people to become His disciples and responsible members of His Church."

Decisions...often verbal assent...are not too difficult to come by, through telephone appeals, "spiritual laws," or altar calls. But a disciple is a different story! Let's not measure our success at the moment of verbal assent. Rather, let's measure success when a transformed life is identified, incorporated into the local church, and becomes a reproducing member of the Body of Jesus Christ. Let's measure success six months to five years later, when that person is incorporated into the Body and living as a disciple should live...in fellowship with Christ, a responsible part in the local church, and walking as a Christian should walk in this world.

2. Question: IS "HERE'S LIFE AMERICA" EFFECTIVE EVANGELISM?

What are the facts? The Institute for American Church Growth researched some of the cities where "Here's Life" was held and talked to some of those involved.

At the front of the Indianapolis effort was the West Morris Street Free Methodist Church, pastored by Rev. Donald Riggs. This is a fine, growing church, with a compassion to see lost people found. The pastor is effective and is leading his people in enlarged ministry and outreach. The lay leadership in the church is outstanding. This church and pastor were selected by Campus Crusade as a model and are featured in a new promotional film for "Here's Life."

In researching the facts with Pastor Riggs, we found, as a part of "Here's Life America," that the church had made over 6,000 phone calls... 362 people made a decision... 20 attended one or more Bible studies. When I asked how many of those people who had made decisions were now (five months later) members of the church, the answer was "Zero"! Effective evangelism? Hardly.

This is not to say there were not benefits. The main value of this emphasis, as identified by the pastor, was in training the lay people. This church, because of its concern for people outside of Jesus Christ, will reap some reward. They have devised their own strategy of using the trained people in an outreach program along with using a "selected prospect list" gained from this program.

The Hope Church was also a significant leader in the Indianapolis emphasis. In conversation with the pastor, I inquired about the facts... nearly 7200 calls were made by 140 trained lay leaders. The "spiritual laws" were shared with 1987... 525 prayed to receive Christ... 72 enrolled for Bible Study... "about," said the pastor, "20 are now members of the church." When I asked for a "guesstimate" concerning the previous church relatedness of the 525 who made a decision, his response was that the vast majority had had some kind of previous church identification. Of the 20 who are now members of the Hope Church, four-fifths of them had previous church affiliations.

The Glendale Church of God is located in Indianapolis. The experience with "Here's Life America" as reported by Assistant Pastor Rev. Jim Martin is that "the approach is 'shot-gunnish'—you really don't hit anything; it is like shooting at a cloud. Laymen felt that in the first week 'things went great,' but the second week callers began reporting that something was wrong. Word had gotten around the neighborhood, people were hanging up on callers, others said they resented the call." The third week was as bad or worse, reported Martin, as resistance continued to build.

The report of resistance and resentment was verified by phone callers from other churches. Is it possible that this approach may build resistance instead of responsiveness, therefore making people more difficult to reach at a later time? I don't know. But the subject should be investigated.

In considering the question, "Is 'Here's Life' effective evangelism?" we spot-checked another area. The South Calgary Community Church, pastored by Rev. Frank Berg, averages about 300 in worship and is located in Calgary. In that city, "Here's Life America" (Canada) was held the last two weeks of April and the first week of May, 1976. For the campaign, this church trained 55 workers, of which 37 participated. Approximately 2300 phone calls were made, the "spiritual laws" shared with 397. Of those 397, 100 people made a "decision." Of these decisions, 1 came to Bible Study. How many are part of the church six months later? "Zero." Effective evangelism?

This same church conducted a massive follow-up three months after the initial thrust. Every person who had received a booklet (about 300), was personally called on in a follow-up visit. The results? No one incorporated into the church. (Three people visited one worship service.)

In Edmonton, a city of approximately 500,000, 63 churches in the area participated in "Here's Life America" (Canada). The budget for the event was $75,000 (approximately $70,000 was spent). 1700 people were trained. By the end of the campaign 1009 decisions had been registered. Approximately 250 attended one or more Bible Studies.

How many of these decisions are now part of a local church? No one knows! In seeking that answer, I checked with ten of the 63 participating churches. None could report any new people incorporated into the Body. Let's speculate for a moment and assume that each of the other cooperating churches incorporated at least one new person into the Body. The cost per new member would be $1,320.75. On that basis, it would cost $416,036,000.00 to reach Edmonton (based on Glenmary research figures). One must ask, not only is it effective evangelism, but is it good stewardship?

"Here's Life" publicity spotlighted Philadelphia where *"10,000 laymen were trained...and met the challenge and contacted 296,500 people personally."*

The Institute, in researching "Here's Life America" in Philadelphia, Pennsylvania, assigned an independent researcher some months later to obtain facts concerning its effectiveness in evangelism.

After repeated attempts to meet with Crusade leaders to secure factual data, the researcher gave up the project because of Crusade's unwillingness to cooperate in making information available. It was learned, however, that the emphasis for which Campus Crusade promoted "Here's Life America" to the Philadelphia churches (that was, reaching Philadelphia for Christ) had turned dramatically and leadership is now saying the purpose was to motivate and train lay people. It was also learned that of the approximately 430 churches which participated, a highly selected list of 20 is being used in a proposed article promoting the project. One pastor, who wished to remain anonymous, told us, "There's no question that 'Here's Life' missed its mark completely in terms of evangelizing Philadelphia for Christ."

For a broader perspective on the total impact of "Here's Life" in a city-wide campaign, the Institute for American Church Growth sent a random sample of 200 surveys to Protestant churches in Indianapolis and 200 to Fresno,

---

SURVEY CARD

1. What is the membership of your congregation?_____
2. Did your church cooperate in the Indianapolis "Here's Life America" emphasis? YES   NO
3. If "NO," why not? _____
   _____ _____ (go to #14)
4. If "YES," how many of your lay people were trained in the program?
5. As part of "Here's Life," how many telephone calls were made into the community from your church?_____
6. How many people had the spiritual laws explained to them by telephone?_____
7. How many of these made a decision to accept Christ?_____
8. How many of those who made a decision began the Bible study?_____
9. How many of those who began the Bible study completed it?_____
10. Did callers see any increase in resistance of those being called, as the campaign progressed? YES   NO
11. Is your church presently involved in an organized continuation of the "Here's Life" program? YES   NO
12. Of the people who were trained in your church, how many are actively involved in continuing their calling program?_____
13. As a direct result of the "Here's Life" emphasis, how many are now new members of your church?_____ Of these new members, how many had had no previous association with any church?_____ How many of the new members came into your church through "transfer?"_____
14. If you had it to do over again, would you want to be a cooperating church in "Here's Life?" YES   NO   Why? _____
15. What are your positive and/or negative comments on "Here's Life America?"

California, where "Here's Life" campaigns had been held six and eight months previously. (See "Survey Questions" above.) At press time, all surveys had not been returned, but patterns were apparent and consistent among reporting churches:

Question #2: 30.9% of the churches in the communities participated in "Here's Life America"; 69.1% did not.

Question #4: 823 people were trained in the "Here's Life" program.

Question #5: 28,976 telephone calls were made during the campaign.

Question #6: 5,991 people had the spiritual laws explained to them.

Question #7: 1,665 people made a decision to accept Christ.

Question #8: 242 people who made a decision began the "Here's Life" Bible Study program.

Question #9: 101 people who began the Bible Study, completed the program.

Question #10: 41.2% of the callers noted an increased resistance by those being called; 58.8% noted no increased resistance.

Question #11: 29.4% of the churches have some kind of continuation of the "Here's Life" program; 70.6% of the churches do not.

Question #12: 114 of the 823 people trained in the program are now actively involved in a continuation of the calling program.

Question #13: 55 people are now members of a church because of the "Here's Life" program. 23 of those 55 transferred from another church or had had some kind of previous involvement with another church.

Question #14: Of the churches who participated in "Here's Life America," 52.9% said they would participate again, if asked; 41.2% said they would not participate again; 5.9% were not sure.

Random comments from those who did participate include:

"Brought about a great unity in local church and among denominations."

"A reasonable impact, good training, fantastic opportunity."

"A good effort to expose the community to the Gospel."

"Training is excellent."

"The main benefit seemed to be the training of workers. I have negative feelings about the method of contact and results of those whom we called."

"It helped train and mobilize Christians. No relationships were established between soul winner and new convert. We learned. We are now doing 'friendship evangelism.' No more cold turkey!"

"Its objectives were realized: 'Place interested people in contact with trained workers.' Unfortunately, many thought the purpose was to build the church."

"No new church membership was realized, as had been anticipated by the workers. There was a great feeling in the end that this effort was good work, but also work in vain."

Random comments from those who did not participate include:

"I question any serious lasting results."

"Information did not reach me."

"Didn't know what it was."

"We're a rural church. I'm not convinced this type of evangelism is effective for us."

"Not impressed with long-term benefits."

"Too costly and Madison-Avenue-like."

"I talked to laity and clergy who participated and they did not indicate it brought many people to Christ."

Is "Here's Life America" effective evangelism? One of the consistent positive results given by participating pastors in the survey was the training of laity in evangelism. Two questions must subsequently be asked:

First—"Do the laity, who were trained, continue to use their training?"

Results from the Indianapolis and Fresno surveys give us some clues. Approximately 10% of all those trained were continuing their calling program, according to the pastors. This figure varied by churches with some reporting no continuation and other churches reporting greater involvement.

In Canada, we verbally surveyed approximately 50 lay people representing 8 churches who had been trained during "Here's Life." No one had won anyone to Christ six months after the campaign.

These two samples were small and perhaps not representative. Hopefully additional facts and broader sampling will reveal just the opposite to be true.

Second—"If the training given to lay leaders was unsuccessful in making disciples and responsible members when applied through their church's involvement in "Here's Life," what evidence is there that these trained lay people will meet with greater success in the future?"

Is "Here's Life" effective evangelism? If one agrees with the Church Growth definition of making disciples and responsible members, the answer is fairly obvious. The staggering "shrinkage" between those who respond to the "spiritual laws" and those who were incorporated into the Body graphically portrays its ineffectiveness—less than four (3.3%) of every 100 "decisions" are now active members of any church; and 42% of these came by transfer.

3. Question: HOW DOES "HERE'S LIFE" VIEW THE CHURCH?

The Church Growth point of view takes a high view of the Church: the Church is absolutely essential. It is not *a* Body of Christ; it is *the* Body of Christ; not just *a* bride, but *the* bride of Christ.

The Church is held to be the central part of God's plan for

the salvation and discipling of men and nations. New converts must not only believe in Jesus Christ, but must become responsible members of the Church. The Bible requires it. If we take the Bible seriously, we cannot hold any other point of view. Becoming a Christian means becoming part of the Body. In fact, unless believers become part of the Church, personified through the local congregation, the reality of their belief must be questioned. This is the high view of the Church as seen through Church Growth Eyes. A low view of the Church is that whether or not you belong to the Church is more or less a matter of choice. If you like it you belong; if you don't, you don't.

How is the Church viewed by "Here's Life America"? This is difficult to determine, as I have read and reread promotional material from Campus Crusade. Looking for clues, I find one headline which says, *"Involvement of Pastors, Laymen Crucial to Campaign's Success."* So it is clear that "using" the church is essential for success. Bruce Cook, Director of "Here's Life America," writes "What is needed to bring 'Here's Life' to your community? Only a few truly committed individuals..." In the same article he writes, "Committed nuclei of fewer than six individuals organized and led 'I Found It' Campaigns in most of the cities conducting campaigns this Spring." From this I conclude that "Here's Life" is not a campaign which comes to a city at the invitation of churches, who work together in a cooperative endeavor. Rather, the inference is "Here we are. If you are a truly committed church you will certainly be a part." As one pastor put it, "They asked us to drop everything we were doing; if we didn't participate, our priorities were wrong." Or, as Bright told the "Praise Celebration" at Anaheim, "After seeing this miracle [of "Here's Life America"] there is only one hindrance to reaching the world—lack of availability and commitment."

Thinking back to the slide-tape presentation for "Here's Life," which I saw some months ago, I remember looking in vain for how decisions are incorporated into a local church. The slide-tape talked of "follow-up," but incorporation into the Body was not mentioned. In the newer 20-minute color film promoting the program, there is also a conspicuous absence of incorporation of decisions into the participating churches. From a Church Growth viewpoint, incorporation into the Body, as previously stated, is of utmost importance.

An interesting perspective to this issue surfaced nationally in *Newsweek* magazine, September 6, 1976. An article entitled "Politics from the Pulpit" stated, "Last winter [Billy] Graham told Bright to remove his name as a supporter of Bright's latest crusade—a massive campaign called 'Here's Life America' through which Bright intends to 'evangelize' the United States by the end of this year, and the entire world by 1980. What most worried Graham are indications that Bright's organization, which also operates in 83 foreign countries, 'has become almost a denomination by itself, in competition with the churches.'"

It would be helpful to know how Campus Crusade views the Church, not only in theory, but also in actual practice.

4. Question: DOES "HERE'S LIFE" SWIRL IN A "FOG" OF PROMOTION AND PROPAGANDA?

"Fog" is defined as a veil, which obscures the facts, confuses what is with what is hoped for, and generally blurs reality.

In front of me is the newest eight-page color promotional piece from Campus Crusade. Frankly, I have difficulty distinguishing between facts, partial facts, and fiction. This is not to point the finger at only one group, for I find that many Christian organizations confuse fact with fiction ...reality with fantasy. This is an easy thing to do and I have been guilty of the same thing. I find it necessary to constantly check myself and verify that I am seeing and presenting the picture from its multi-faceted perspective.

When we do not, a wide credibility gap opens and hinders growth of His Body.

Consider this statement of Bright, who calls "Here's Life America" the *"Greatest spiritual harvest in the history of the Church. 100 times —yes, 1000 times —greater than anything I have ever seen or read about in the almost 2000-year-old history of the Church."* Over-kill? I think so.

I can hardly believe he has never heard of the phenomenal growth of the early Church...or of the rise of the Protestant Reformation...the Wesleyan movement...or more currently the movement of God in Africa, where, south of the Sahara, the continent is becoming substantially Christian...or Indonesia, where a great discipling process is taking place among long established Moslems.

The Church of Jesus Christ is advancing on many fronts. Rejoice in all such progress. However, it is, to me, a serious misrepresentation to claim *"Here's Life America"* is a *thousand times greater than anything in the almost two-thousand year history of the Church."* That's FOG!

Are there other examples of fog? Here is a claim that "Here's Life" is *"...just the beginning of a movement that will sweep across America, revolutionizing the lives of tens of millions..."* What does the beginning of a movement mean? A new denomination? Or a historic revival? Or what? And how many really are tens of millions? Fog is using vague generalities. Fog is making claims that lack substance.

Try this one: *"Here's Life, Birmingham revolutionized me and my entire church"* says the Rev. John Crow of Avondale Presbyterian Church in Birmingham. I rejoice with you, pastor, but I am curious to know how you and your church have been revolutionized. What were the conditions before the revolution? How many were revolutionized? How long did the revolution last? Has the revolution resulted in any significant number of formerly non-Christians becoming disciples and responsible members of your church? Until some of these questions are answered, it's FOG!

The "Here's Life" campaign in the United States is projected to be completed within this year.

The claim was made by Bright, at the conclusion of "Here's Life Southern California" that "...here in the United States the Great Commission will be fulfilled by the end of this year."

Will the Great Commission have been fulfilled—even in Southern California? What are the facts?

"Here's Life," at the "celebration rally" for Southern California, claimed 515,000 households had been contacted, 98,600 heard the spiritual laws, and 27,600 made decisions. Now compare the total population in Southern California—11,594,215—with the 515,000 contacts made by "Here's Life": 4.4%. Then compare the total unreached people in Southern California—9,312,400—with the 27,600 decisions: 0.296%.

Let's assume that we can generalize the results of the Indianapolis/Fresno survey to Southern California (3.3 active church members for every 100 decisions). That means 911 new people in churches or less than 1 new member for each participating church (950); of which 381 would have transferred from one church to another. It becomes very clear that the Great Commission has not been fulfilled in Southern California...it's just begun.

5. Question: IS "HERE'S LIFE" WORTH THE EFFORT?

Positive values can be identified:

1. *Something is being done...* to communicate a positive Christian message by media. It's one thing to talk about fulfilling the Great Commission, but it is another thing to do something about it. Until hard, bold plans are made and carried out, not much evangelism is accomplished. Campus Crusade is doing something. They are not theorists in their ivory tower discussing what might be done. They are

where the battle rages, where the bullets are real, in the media market place. Such Herculean efforts and vision should be commended.

2. *It is their best effort to date.* Mass evangelism in America, in recent years, has been sterile in its methodology. One man...large crowds..."Just as I am"...decision cards to churches...next crusade, etc. "Here's Life America" is a creative new way to touch people. Not only is the approach new and fresh, but one senses that Campus Crusade is building upon both failures and successes of the past for a more effective approach in the future.

3. *Evangelism has moved closer to the local church.* This is laudatory. Research indicates that the greater the gap between the local church and the evangelistic effort, the less fruit will remain. "Here's Life America" has taken steps toward closing that gap. The coordination between evangelistic efforts and local churches will result in more lasting fruit. This is a positive step forward for evangelism in America.

4. *Lay people are being trained and involved.* "Here's Life" combines the impersonal media with the personal follow-up. To accomplish this, lay people are being trained and utilized. I hope the training received will be practiced long after the crusade is finished. In some cases, I believe it will. While I would like to see better training, not in terms of *methods*, but *goals*, one must affirm the training of large numbers of lay people for evangelistic efforts.

5. *High visibility is being achieved.* The power of media is considerable, and the concentrated efforts to raise the consciousness level of non-Christians to possibilities in Christ is a positive contribution. How many of those who see the message, while not at the point of a Christian commitment, will unwittingly take and store in their "psyche" the possibility of a new life in Christ? A difficult question to answer; however, I must conclude that a reservoir of Christian truth in the minds of many people could

be used by the Holy Spirit when these people are faced with a time of need. High visibility of the Christian message is certainly an important contribution of this program.

In looking at "Here's Life America" through Church Growth eyes, what do we see—an "electronic gospel blimp," or a demonstration of a powerful way to use media for Christ?

Perhaps some of both.

The concern of the Institute for American Church Growth and of Campus Crusade is to see the Great Commission accomplished in the shortest possible time in the most effective way. As Church Growth is being structured into more and more denominations and local congregations across America, inquiries have been made to us by pastors and denominational executives concerning the relationship between "Here's Life America" and Church Growth. We, too, have been concerned with this question and thus have endeavored to seek honest answers. At this point, and with the current emphasis of "Here's Life," we must conclude that there is no substantial relationship between the two. This is not to say a mutually supportive relationship is not possible, or desirable. Indeed it is.

A good starting point would be for an enlarged study conducted by independent researchers, honestly evaluating results. Thereby, using this research, eliminate the weakness, build on the strength, and restructure the program so it becomes effective evangelism and an instrument which could be used of God for the growth of His Church.

As we in the Church continue to grow in the understanding of our role in fulfilling Christ's Great Commission, we must move forward in significant new strides to win men, make disciples and responsible members of His Church, thereby glorifying Jesus Christ, who indeed is leading us into our communities and into all the world.

Seven Characteristics of a Growing Church

BY REV. KEN PARKER

The book of Acts has been called "The Tale of Three Cities." It begins with the mighty wonders in the city of Jerusalem. Then the activity shifts to the almost unknown city of Antioch. As the book of Acts closes, the center of witness seems to be the city of Rome, where Paul writes his stirring epistles to the churches.

The church at Antioch is a particularly interesting study in church growth. Going back to this center of Christian activity, a great deal can be learned about the growth and vitality of this early church and its relevance to our churches today.

Antioch was the location of Paul's home church. It was through this body of believers that a world-wide missionary effort first began and has never ceased. From this body of believers Paul received much inspiration and support. This church was used by the Spirit of God to commission Paul and send him out for that special ministry to which the Lord had called him. Let's look at seven characteristics of the church at Antioch, which seem to be common to growing churches through history and today.

Rev. Parker is pastor of the Berean Church, Spokane, Washington.

1. A STRONG COMMITMENT TO WORSHIP

The Antioch church was deeply committed to offering the praise of their hearts to God. "While they were worshipping and fasting, the Holy Spirit said, 'Set apart for me Barnabas and Saul for the work to which I have called them.'"

And it was said of the churches in Macedonia that they "First gave themselves to the Lord" (II Cor. 8:5), following this same pattern of a worshipful church.

There are many aspects to worship, but perhaps the basis upon which all other forms of worship are built is prayer. A living, growing church is a praying church; a church that believes in and practices the highest form of worship-prayer.

A commitment to prayer as a congregation does not mean selecting one night of the week as prayer meeting night. Rather, it involves the leadership and the membership of the church in their commitment to personal growth through personal prayer. It involves small prayer-care groups, instruction and study on the subject of prayer, daily involvement in regular prayer for one another and for the growth of the church. Public sharing in prayer comes after first developing a strong personal commitment to prayer by each member of the congregation.

A strong church is a church committed to worship, a church whose first thoughts are of their Lord.

2. A STRONG COMMITMENT TO OUTREACH

This does not simply mean presenting the gospel within the confines of the church building; it involves community penetration.

The church in Antioch was born through a community penetration project. Acts 11:20, 21 tells us "Some of them, however, men of Cyprus and Cyrene, went to Antioch and began to speak to Greeks also, telling them the good news about the Lord Jesus. The Lord's hand was with them, and a great number of people believed and turned to the Lord."

What would have happened if the believers of the dispersion had settled in Antioch, rented a building, and placed a sign out front... *"The First Church of the Persecuted Saints of Jesus Christ...Morning Services 11:00 A.M. Evening Services 7:00 P.M., Midweek Prayer Meeting 7:00 P.M. Wednesdays"*? The people in Antioch would probably have stayed away in droves. The community would not have been touched with the gospel; a vital growing church would not have come into existence.

Paul carried with him the practice that he may very well have learned from his early associations with the saints at Antioch. Acts 20:20 tells us that he went from house to house preaching the gospel. Acts 17:17 shows us that Paul went daily into the market place to share Christ.

Evangelism is the cornerstone of the local church. It is not some optional plan, but an essential priority.

The commitment to outreach not only includes penetration of the local community, but involves commitment to penetrating the world community for Christ. To restate it, a growing church is a church with a world vision. It is a church with a strong commitment to missions world wide—starting next door.

The Antioch church was also a world vision church. They were one of the first sending and supporting mission boards recorded in scripture. In Acts 13:3 we note, "So after they had fasted and prayed, they placed their hands on them [Barnabas and Saul] and sent them off."

Later in Acts 14:27, they anxiously heard the report from their missionaries regarding the opening of the door of faith to the Gentiles.

It is a shame to see the many para-church organizations doing the work that actually belongs to the local church. These organizations exist, primarily, because most churches have forfeited their privilege of commitment to outreach.

A growing church is one that accepts its role as *the* biblical agency for reaching the world for Christ.

3. A STRONG COMMITMENT TO EDIFICATION OF THE SAINTS

Some call it discipleship, others call it Christian education, others have their own names. Whatever, it involves the basic provision of building the spiritual strength of the body of believers. Inward growth is the necessary complement of outward growth.

Of the Antioch Church we read: "They preached the Lord Jesus Christ..." (Acts 11:2) "They taught the Word..." (Acts 11:26, and Acts 15:35) "They were exhorted..." (Acts 11:23) "Paul and Barnabas continued in Antioch, teaching and preaching the Word of the Lord with many others " (Acts 15:35). Biblical preaching and study is the foundation for internal growth and the development of Spirit-controlled men and women.

It might be that the so-called "Timothy principle" was first seen in operation by Paul at his home church. "The things you have heard me say in the presence of many witnesses entrust to reliable men who will be qualified to teach others" (II Tim. 2:2).

The Antioch church certainly developed Spirit-controlled disciples. We read these thrilling words in Acts 11:26, "So for a whole year Barnabas and Saul met with the church, and taught numbers of people. The disciples were first called Christians at Antioch."

What a testimony of the results of discipleship. The world looked upon these saints and said, "They are Christians...." Their lives were reflective of the life of Christ. They not only spoke of Christ, but they were Christ.

4. A STRONG COMMITMENT TO PEOPLE

When a visitor walks into the church, will he feel and sense that the people in the congregation love the Lord and each other? And will he sense that these people love him?

Of the church in Antioch it is recorded, "Then the disciples, each according to his ability, decided to provide help for the brothers living in Judea" (Acts 11:29).

One significant element of a people-oriented ministry is a real interest and commitment to the family. Do we fragment the family and drive them further apart, or do we seek to strengthen the bonds of the family?

Ephesians chapters five and six certainly show the importance of the family to the proper witness of the gospel.

A growing church must also be a caring church. They must care about the physical and social needs of people in addition to their spiritual needs. How often does the church today fulfill the description James gives in his epistle; "Suppose a brother or sister is without clothes and daily food. If one of you says to him, 'Go, I wish you well, keep warm and well fed,' but does nothing about his physical needs, what good is it?" (James 2:15, 16).

The Holy Spirit through James is showing that a living body of believers must care for one another in a very human and tangible way.

5. A STRONG COMMITMENT TO GROWTH AS A GOAL

The church at Antioch, as we have noted, fasted and prayed and then sent out missionaries. They were interested in the results of the missionary ministry of Saul and Barnabas. Later they sent Silas and John Mark on their way. All of this would tend to indicate that they had made growth a distinct part of their goal as a church.

It may well be that Paul was reflecting the spirit of the church at Antioch when he wrote to the saints at Rome. "It has always been my ambition to preach the gospel where Christ was not known so that I would not be building on someone else's foundation" (Romans 15:20).

In addition to a goal of external growth, our projection must also include a definite plan to reproduce other congregations. Someone has said, "The real fruit of a peach tree is not peaches, but another peach tree." Perhaps it is also true that the ultimate fruit of a church is another church. Certainly Paul saw his primary goal as a church planter, with God giving the increase (I Cor. 3:6). Church planting should be one of the essential aspects of a church's goal to grow.

There are actually some groups of believers who have been deceived by the enemy into thinking that growth is wrong or undesirable, and that the desire to grow is especially wrong. But, as we see from Antioch and the records of the early church in Acts, they grew because they desired to grow in fulfillment of their Lord's command.

There are many references in Acts to the actual numbers of those who were saved. There are other references to the great number who responded or who were influenced by a particular moving of the Holy Spirit. The early Christians placed a heavy emphasis on growth of the Body.

6. A STRONG COMMITMENT TO THE POSSIBILITY OF CHANGE.

The church at Jerusalem sent Barnabas in to investigate this new phenomenon they were hearing about in Antioch (Acts 11:22), where some very revolutionary things were being done. The Council of Jerusalem included reports of the strange tendency on the part of the church at Antioch to do things "differently."

But the saints at Antioch were responding to God's revelation of Christ, which Paul was given to preach. They had a desire to follow the leading of the Holy Spirit and worship God in a meaningful way.

Some churches continue to resist exploring such innovations as home Bible study groups, because of the tradition of a midweek service. Others feel that even the times of their services are somewhat sacred; as though God had said, "Thou shalt have thy morning service at 11:00 AM, thy evening service at 7:00 PM."

The apostle Paul was an innovator, not simply to be different, but because he wanted to reach people for Christ. Consider what he says in I Cor. 9:22,23: "To the weak I became weak, to win the weak. I have become all things to all men, so that by all possible means I might save some." Paul was also personally flexible. He says to the Philippians, "I have learned to be content, whatever the circumstances. I know what it is to be in need, and I know what it is to have plenty. I have learned the secret of being content in any and every situation, whether well fed or hungry, whether living in plenty or in want."

Just as the Lord would have individuals be flexible in all circumstances of life, so He would have local churches be able to adjust and change as the needs arise. How those last words of the church have haunted us time and time again: *"We have never done it that way before."*

7. A STRONG COMMITMENT TO SACRIFICE AND FAITHFULNESS

Paul shows loyalty to the church at Antioch when, in Acts 15:36, he asks their permission to go out again on another mission. Certainly, he was following the pattern which was considered proper in that assembly of believers.

The Lord places a high priority on faithfulness. In I Cor. 4:2 we are told, "It is required that those who have been given a trust must prove faithful." Indeed as members of the Body of Christ, we have been given a sacred trust, and the local church has been created by God to be the basis for executing this trust. One cannot be faithful to the trust of the gospel and be unfaithful to the local church.

A growing church is characterized by men and women who are freely giving of their time, their resources and their substance so that Christ might be honored and His ministry advanced. Where there is a growing church there is a church where members give freely and lovingly. There is a spirit of faithfulness and stewardship of time and talents.

In going "back to Antioch" and other growing churches of the New Testament, we see the basis of eternal principles of growth and outreach. Take a look at the growing churches that you know of, and see if you do not see a measure of these same principles at work today.

Growth-Restricting Obstacles: How to Find and Overcome Them

BY JOHN UHLIG

It is not uncommon to see a new congregation, given a vision, a leader and a motivated core of lay people, begin from point zero and grow quite rapidly.[1]

These churches grow because they have dedicated laity excited with the potential of their church and very aware that if their congregation is going to minister to its community, *they* are the ones responsible to God for its effective leadership. In their new setting, these young churches are unencumbered by inhibiting traditions or unproductive programs. A brand new church can usually get off to a flying start!

But for an older congregation, the story is quite different. Usually growth is far from spontaneous and instant success is rare. Growth is slower, there are many discouragements, and patience is a virtue.

The following is a list (based on this writer's personal analysis, experience, and study) of some key "growth-

Rev. Uhlig is senior pastor of the Redeemer Lutheran Church, Redwood City, Cal.

restricting obstacles" which must be understood and overcome for plateaued or declining older congregations to experience renewed growth and outreach.

THE PASTOR-SHEPHERD ROLE

Many older congregations have a very definite view regarding the role of their pastor. He is to shepherd them—that is, serve them. He is there for them—for their needs and their comfort. He leads them beside still waters and makes them lie down in green pastures. He is there to refresh their souls. He is expected to visit them in their home regularly, to call when sick, to counsel when in trouble—for this he is paid. The concept of Ephesians 4:12 is not a part of their tradition, and he is not perceived as a gift from God to train the laity for their ministry. It takes time to get a membership to think of itself in terms of serving rather than being served.

THE "CHURCH-CLUB" ATMOSPHERE

The older congregation once was young. In infancy and adolescence, members had an overriding desire to see the church grow and mature. Members worked long, hard hours making evangelism calls, inviting friends, going house-to-house, knocking on doors. There was a dynamic, a magnetic cohesion, a common goal which knit them into a working fellowship. And success came—growth sufficient to carry on a comfortable program. No need now to work so hard. Take a breather; enjoy the fruits of labor; relax and take your ease in Zion. So the period of relaxation comes, much like semi-retirement. Just enough evangelism work is done to maintain a comfortable attendance level. But it is done mainly by the pastor and a few faithful. "This is the time to enjoy all that we've worked on so zealously—the beautiful sanctuary, the lovely organ, the soft pews; it's their turn." It takes strong leadership and sometimes outside assistance to guide a congregation out of the "country club" mentality and back onto the battlefield of soul-winning.

REARRANGED PRIORITIES

Jesus clearly delineated His priorities for the Church in Matt. 28:19: (1) Evangelizing—"Make disciples of all nations." (2) Baptizing—bringing the blessings Jesus bought on the cross to His people, and leading them in a commitment to His authority and His Word, in a local congregation, in regular worship, study, and service. (3) "Teaching them to observe all things whatsoever I have commanded you..." The Christian is taught, with the purpose of knowing and doing God's will. And the highest and best work a Christian can do is to make disciples.

As congregations grow older, they often unconsciously rearrange their priorities. "#1"—evangelism—may become "#4," or it may be all but shelved.

Sometimes education simply for the sake of education takes over the number one spot. The emphasis may be on music, or building, and this displaces outreach. The priority may be with social action. All these emphases are important, but they must be ranked under the priority found throughout the Scripture emphasizing that "the Son of man is come to seek and to save that which was lost."

In many older churches, fund-raising even can become the number one item. Programs have been developed over the years, and each has become "sacred" in its own right. Each requires funds and more funds. So often it happens that the raising of money becomes the major item of concern at every church board meeting! This is surely a signal that something is wrong!

To grow and expand, the congregation must re-study its priorities and place its programs under the authority of God's Word. This again takes leadership, daring, time and patience. It is not always easy to restore Jesus' priorities for the church to their rightful place.

GENERATION DEGENERATION

As a congregation drifts farther and farther away from the original founders and from their original purposes, a degeneration inevitably takes place. New members are added who share neither the fervor nor the clearly defined goals of the founders. First and second generation children of the founders do not have the old enthusiasm, dedication and zeal.

For such a church, the spiritual fires in its members must be rekindled in youth and adult alike. An easy task? Not at all! Its children and members must be rescued from this "generation degeneration curve," and recommit themselves to the urgency and necessity of reaching those in its ministry area.

THE INFLUENCE OF THE DENOMINATION

Ordinarily the older congregation has been affiliated with a denomination a longer period of time. Inevitably, the influence of the denomination is felt. Where this influence is good, the results in the congregation are positive.

For example, the denomination may maintain a worldwide expanding mission front. It seeks the support of its churches, and this is to be welcomed. The congregation shares in the spreading of the Gospel—the number one priority. Or, the denomination maintains colleges and seminaries for the training of future pastors, missionaries, and Christian day school teachers. The congregation's participation in such efforts are all for the good.

But suppose the denomination has begun to shift its priorities! Social action and political involvement is being advocated. Or, purity of doctrine has become the clarion call. Or, education for the sake of education is championed. Or, suppose the fiscal burden has become heavier and heavier, necessitating endless pleas to the congregations.

What happens is that congregations heeding these pleas and yielding solely to denominational direction begin to rearrange their priorities to suit the denomination. These goals may become the single congregational emphasis, replacing the most worthy goal of discipling men and women at home and around the world.

The pastor-leader may be hard pressed to maintain his and the congregation's denominational loyalty and remain true to the imperatives and priorities of the church. But he must keep the biblical priorities first and organize all his efforts and the resources of the church toward this end.

THE PRIESTHOOD OF BELIEVERS NOT OPERATIVE

The Bible clearly teaches that each Christian is a priest of God in his own right, with all the privileges and the responsibilities of God's priests.[2] He believes that the Holy Spirit has "gifted" him with special abilities to do special work suited to his gifts as determined by the Holy Spirit.[3] He is to discover and use these gifts—as a priest of God in the service of Christ's Church.

However, it is easy for long-established members of older churches to pay only lip-service to this teaching. The drift is to "let George do it," or even "let the pastor do it—that's why we're paying him." Older congregations often have a larger proportion of inactive Christians; ones who have accepted Jesus but have kept Him off the throne in their personal lives. They have yielded intellectually to the claims of Christ as Savior but not as Lord of their lives.

The task of the pastor/leader is to lead these people out of the "reserves" and into active participation and involvement in the Great Commission. This takes understanding, patience, time, instruction, and exhortation. But only spirit-filled Christians "walking in the Spirit" will bring about expansion and growth.

RESISTANCE TO CHANGE AND NEW IDEAS

The older a congregation gets, the more resistance there is to change and new ideas. This concept often has a parallel in the life of an individual as he grows older. He has settled down and become comfortable, and he resists jostling.

But growth and expansion sometimes means changing people, changing programs, and changing ministries; not for the sake of change, but for the sake of effectively ministering to the needs of a changing world. The leader should be prepared for resistance. It's natural. But growth-directed persistence pays off.

THE CONFIRMATION SYNDROME

Some churches and denominations adhere to a custom of confirmation of their children. This involves special instruction for youth in the seventh and eighth grades. The course includes the chief doctrines of Scripture, centering on the atonement through Jesus Christ. Adults desiring to join the church go through a similar course on an adult level, extending fourteen to sixteen sessions.

Christian indoctrination is surely achieved, and this is a strong plus.

However, there are some weaknesses in the system. Confirmation often is looked upon as graduation—as having arrived—having reached the zenith. It can be implied that there is no more to learn and no more for the member to do except attend church service. To be sure, this is not intended, but it often happens.

Youth, having "crammed" and studied for two years of intensive training, seem to be "spiritually tired." They don't flock to the youth programs. Sometimes they are less than excited about worship services and Bible classes. In some cases, they have achieved intellectual understanding without volitional and behavioral commitment. They are not ready for witnessing and disciple-making. The emphasis is so much on indoctrination that they have missed entirely a deep, personal relationship with the living Jesus.

Dropouts among the youth are heavy. A study of this writer's congregation done some years ago showed a 70%

drop-out eight years after confirmation. The parents who "pushed" their children into and through the confirmation years rest on their laurels now that the task is done. They have done their duty. Little more is required of them.

All too often this feeling of "having arrived" also carries through in the adult class. Too many feel that they are at the peak, having climbed the mountain heights of confirmation. It takes effort to get them into Bible classes. To involve them in witnessing and evangelism requires a lot of push-pull. This condition is certainly not conducive to expansion and growth.

To conclude this report with no further statement on the great potential for growth of the older congregation would be at least depressing, at worst incomplete.

The older congregation has many unique pluses which a young congregation often lacks. It has a resource of talent in its membership. It has leadership and often a skilled and experienced staff. It often has money and a good location. Yet the reason many older congregations experience plateaus and/or decline is not their lack of potential. It is most often their inability to focus "church growth eyes" on the number of "growth-restricting obstacles" that often appear as a congregation matures and "grows up."

The problems must be understood and challenged. They must be dedicated to God and resolved. Then the older congregation can once again begin to see growth, outreach, and return to renewed energy for seeing Christ's greatest desire—in the salvation of men and women—become an exciting reality through their congregation.

FOOTNOTES

1. Elmer L. Towns. *America's Fastest Growing Churches* (Nashville: Impact Books, 1972), p. 38
2. I Peter 2: 9–10.
3. I Cor. 12:11

The Apathetic and Bored Church Member

BY JOHN S. SAVAGE

Research Shows that 33% of Church Members Are Inactive

All churches have persons that could be categorized as "active," "less active" and "inactive." The basic premise on which this research project was conceived is that persons move through a series of stages when going from active to inactive participants in the church. While the figures of church growth indicate, for many churches and denominations, substantial decline in membership statistics over the past ten years, most do not show the number of persons who have become inactive yet remained in the membership numbers quoted. Of the churches in this study, it was found that approximately 33% of the congregation membership was in the *"inactive"* category. This study was designed to discover the psychological, relational and emotional dynamics that occur when a church member moves from category "A"—active, to category "B"—less active, to category "C"—inactive.

RESULTS:

■ In the beginning of a movement away from active church involvement, there is very often an incident which produces some kind of anxiety, making the individual feel uncomfortable and giving him/her a sense of being "off

---

Dr. Savage is founder and president of LEAD Consultants, Pittsford, New York.

balance." The initial reaction to this anxiety is to find a comfortable state again. Ninety-five percent of the persons interviewed in categories "B" and "C" could recall quite clearly what the event was, when it happened, and could express strong feelings about it.

■ What triggers off the anxiety, making the parishioner so uncomfortable that he or she becomes angry enough to leave the church? There appear to be three signficant precipitants that bring these feelings of anxiety. They are, in order of their intensity: 1) conflict with the pastor, 2) conflict with another family member, 3) conflict with another church member.

■ When anxiety reaches the stage of acute discomfort the anxiety is transformed to anger. When anger develops, the individual exhibits agitated behavior, becoming more aggressive or withdrawn. If the individual finds no resolution, the result is that he moves farther away from the setting in which the anxiety-producing situation is located. This is noted quite clearly in the frequency of worship, working on committees, and financial giving. Ninety-six percent of those in category "A" had made a financial pledge to the church, while only 23% of category "C" pledged. Ninety-five percent of the "A's" served on committees, 24% of the "B's" served on committees, 0% of the "C's" served on committees. Worship attendance, however, is the initial behavior affected and is one of the most sensitive indicators of what is happening to the parishioner.

■ The inactive members back off from their church relationships, but do not re-engage in any other congregation. Less than 1% could be called "church hoppers." They still consider it "their church."

■ Each of those interviewed in the inactive group indicated that no one from the church had ever come to find out why they were losing interest or had dropped out. Almost one-third of this group visibly cried during the interview, indicating the intensity of unresolved feelings.

▪ As the individual moves away from the church, there is expressed a considerable amount of grief mixed with anger; yet longing to return to a comfortable state.

▪ In this study, there were no significant differences between the active and inactive members regarding theological issues.

▪ After persons have dropped out, they wait six to eight weeks to see if anyone will come to them to find out why they had left. During that period there is a type of holding pattern—a non-engaging behavior—that takes place. They do not reinvest the time in any other area, but passively wait. If no help comes, they begin to reinvest their time in other organizations, such as scouts, social clubs, as well as recreational activities, such as camping. By the time they have reinvested their time, much of the intense feeling has subsided and a mental reorientation begins to take place creating a greater distance between themselves and the church. However, at least 50% of the inactive members still maintain a Christian perspective in their life, read the Bible, use their faith to help make decisions, and see themselves as servants of God.

▪ A final chapter in the study is devoted to comments by the author on his personal impressions of how a pastor and/or lay visitor should encounter the apathetic and bored church member. A systematic view of visitation techniques is also included.

Dr. Savage concludes his study: *"It is clear from this research that the Church of Jesus Christ, if it is to be an effective instrument to its own membership, needs to sensitize itself to what is going on in the lives of its own people. Until that occurs, there will be many persons who will leave the active ranks of our local churches.*

The Church and the Changing Community

BY TOM WOLF

"I would personally rather believe differently, but I cannot escape the mounting evidence that the pastor heads the list of factors common to growing churches in America... Show me a rapidly growing church, and I will show you a dynamic leader whom God is using to make it happen."
Your Church Can Grow—Wagner. Regal Books, Glendale, CA, 1976

Why one would want to believe differently or escape the evidence is not clear. But to those of us who are pastors, who are in the trenches and on the battlefield, our experience confirms the documentation. Show me a growing church and I will show you a man of God, called of God, leading the people of God into the work of God. When God convenes a mission, God calls a man.

This is true at a national or international level. It is equally true at the local congregational level. God prepares the soil. God readies a people. And then He calls a man. If

---

Rev. Tom Wolf is highly qualified to speak on the growth of the church in the changing community. When Tom arrived at the "Church on Brady Street" in East Los Angeles, it was on the verge of closure and death. Today the church is alive and growing in exciting new ways. Rev. Tom Wolf is featured in the film "...and They Said It Couldn't Be Done!"

your church is going to grow, pastor, it is because God is calling you as the one final condition. Of course, laymen must be sufficiently motivated, principles of growth must be properly understood and applied. But growth will seldom occur unless you, the pastor, are convinced that it is God's will that your church grow, and His lost children are found.

When God convenes a work, He creates in the heart of His people a desperation, a longing, a thirst, a craving for deliverance (Exod. 1 & 3:7) When I came to "The Church on Brady Street" God had sovereignly prepared His people for change and for growth. They were desperate.

The weeds outside the building rested their leafy elbows on the four-foot-high window sills. The building had not been painted in 17 years. In a sanctuary that seats over 500, we had one mid-week service with only six people—three of those being myself, my wife and our infant son. One Sunday evening we had 13. The sanctuary carpeting of an original rich rose was now a putrid pink. At the entrance of the sanctuary the carpeting was worn away completely, the matting was shredded, and the bare concrete smirked up at those entering the church. The buildings were defeated. But worse than that, the buildings were the badge of a defeated people. With grim courage some brothers and sisters held on. With unbelievable tenacity, a remnant remained faithful.

God was getting ready to do a work. And any time God does a work He prepares for that work by creating hunger in the hearts of His people. There was a group which sat down and wept by the waters of "the Babylon of nongrowth." And there they remembered Zion—the days when they *had* grown, the years past when the sanctuary sang with full pews, the halls of the education building ran with children and the parking lots were full and overflowing. But now things were different. On the willows of shrinking attendance they hung up their lyres. Their tormentors mocked, saying: "Sing to us one of the songs of Zion—a song of the church triumphant."

The community had changed. The neighbors were different. The old members were not driving in any more. It was the late '60 s when sex was free, speech was foul, Viet Nam was fermenting and the church was tired. Oh God! How could anyone sing a song to the Lord in such a land?

But it was there. Not exactly a song; it was more of a cry, a yearning, a deep devout gasp. It came from bended knees and oppressed backs. It came from the heart and it ended in heaven. "If I forget you, O Jerusalem, let my right hand wither" (Psalm 137:5, RSV). They resolutely refused to forget the days when God had blessed, when people were being reborn, when the fellowship was sweet and when the church was growing.

And then, God called a man...the final condition. The key factor...the remaining fact. And what a sight! Like a herdsman from the hills. Like a fignipper from the barn. Our people wanted a bilingual man—I spoke only English (and had trouble with that at times). Our people wanted a mature man with experience—I was 24 and had never pastored. Our people wanted a man with his degrees—I had not even completed seminary. But there was a meeting ground: they prayed and I prayed. They called. I came. And God began a new thing on Brady Street.

I cannot escape the fact that the pastor heads the list of factors common to growing churches in America. We pastors are not perfect. How well we all know that from the trenches. How I have wept because of my stupidity, hardness of heart, dumbness, insensitivity. But praise God—even the men of old were men with a nature like ours (James 5:7–18). My mother used to say, "God gets a lot of good licks from some mighty crooked sticks."

If God does a work in our congregations, if our church is going to grow, it is going to be because we grow. Because we fall on our faces and cry to the Lord. Because we wrestle

Him and refuse to acknowledge the dawn until He blesses us. Because we refuse for our people and His flock not to grow. "If I forget you, O Jerusalem, let my right hand wither." And if it's withered—Lord, restore it. Heal me, Lord. The pastor...the final condition.

"Lord, make your church grow. And may my hand wither if it doesn't." That's where church growth begins.

US News & World Report, in a recent article "Who Really Runs Washington," noted: "The fact is, politicians come and go in Washington...but it is the 'Super Bureaucrats' who stay forever—and it is they who really run the Government. Elected by nobody, The 'Super Bureaucrats' form a thin layer of anonymity between the rank-and-file government. Elected by nobody, the 'Super Bureaucrats' form with each new administration. This group heads federal offices, speeds or delays action by government, promotes or sidetracks bills in Congress, and tells Presidents what they can and can't do..."

One might well ask: "Who really runs the Church?" While pastors come and go in most local churches, it is often the "Super Bureaucrats" who stay forever—and it is they who really run the local church. Who are the "Super Bureaucrats" of the church that form the layer of anonymity between pastor and people, between the rank-and-file and the new minister who brings his new administration? Who is the group that can speed or delay action in the congregation, promote or sidetrack new ideas and tell pastors what they can and can't do? The answer, in its simplest form, is **lay leadership.** Remember US News & World Report? "It is the 'Super-Bureaucrats' who stay forever." That's the key: **longevity.** Pastors come and go. The ones over the years who have to really carry the load of the congregation and form the bulwark of stability, the cornerstone upon which the church is built, are the local lay leadership.

And how patient and godly they are! I will never forget that Wednesday night business meeting during my first summer as pastor. I wanted to start a street ministry. My heart was burdened with others at the pleading needs crawling the streets of our changing community. We had found a place to rent. Volunteers seemed eager. Some gifts had already come in above regular giving. But there was need of congregational confirmation and undergirding. It was business meeting time.

As the discussion went on, something seemed to be going wrong. There was hesitation beyond needed clarification. Something was brewing. There was clearing of throats, shifting of shoulders, shaking of heads and knowing glances. I felt that undefined layer of resistance-delaying action.

Let me share what we did. I interrupted the conversation, blurting out: "Let's stop a minute. I sense we need to pray." Why did I do that? I don't know. It's not in Robert's Rules. But I groaned deep within, with a yearning I cannot fully express. I wanted to weep. I wanted to run off alone and cry out to God. I wanted to bring a healing ointment to wounded lives. "Brothers and sisters," I started, "there is something that I want to share with you before we pray. I sense some of you are afraid...afraid of this new experience...afraid that this project may fail...and....," I trailed off. It was suddenly clear in my heart, in my head, in my soul. I choked. Silence like that of an empty country house filled the meeting. Finally, I went on: "And I sense that somewhere deep down, some of you are afraid that if this project fails, you might be left alone in this community to pick up the pieces. You will have to face your friends, family, long-time acquaintances. And you're afraid— though I know you'd probably never say so—that just about the time we failed, I would receive a 'call' to go somewhere else." The silence got louder. "Know this, beloved. If this project ever happens and succeeds—we succeed together. And if it fails, we'll pick up the pieces—together."

Then we prayed. As I lead in prayer, the central theme seemed to be: "Lord, we don't even need this project. But, Lord make us one. Teach us to lay down our lives, our projects, ourselves for each other." When the prayer finished, Brother Sam, a 62-year-old deacon, who had been at Brady 21 years, stood. He moved that we do the project. It was seconded and passed. And the project failed.

But we picked up the pieces—together.

Ever so gently we learned something then. It's been 7 years. They learned that I was more interested in their problems, their perspective, them as people than in my projects. And I learned that Jesus was right again. "The sheep follow the good shepherd because they know his voice." And a stranger they simply will not follow, but will flee from because they do not know the voice of strangers. Too many of us, as pastors, have been like Washington politicians, just passing through. Our calling is not to light for awhile, but to lay down our life. It takes time for people to learn our voice—perhaps two to three years. That's when our work really begins. But for too many, that's when it ends. Longevity is the crying need in the pastorate today. May God give us men who will forget their career, their potential, their future. Let God take care of that. May we see men willing to lay down their lives for a single fold. Men who will stop fretting about themselves and feed their sheep. Men who will strengthen the sickly, heal the diseased, bind up the broken, bring back the scattered.

No wonder many cannot look to their pastors, when the pastors keep deserting the flock. Problems come and pastors go. God bring the day when pastors will stay and problems will go. Pastoral longevity: one of the keys to significant church growth.

How to Build High Morale in Your Church
BY REV. CHARLES MYLANDER

One of the essential conditions a pastor must be responsible for in a growing church is high morale. It forms a repetitive cycle...high morale is conducive to church growth, which results in higher morale, which is a factor in greater growth...etc....It happens time after time...as more and more people find new life in Christ a growing sense of excitement permeates the congregation.

Whenever a growth momentum begins to build, wise leaders will keep it going. Rather than trying to consolidate their gains, the pastor and influential lay leaders will work to increase the growth rate. They know that morale and momentum work hand in hand. They also know that a stagnant, non-growing church is usually a church with low morale.

Growth is not a simple option for a local church concerned with high morale...it is a necessity. Think of an airplane in flight. In the instant that the forward thrust ceases, inevitable decline begins. Unless a restoration of power propels the plane to recover the lost altitude, disaster looms ahead. High morale can provide fuel for the Holy Spirit to thrust a church forward.

Rev. Mylander is Assistant Pastor of the Rose Drive Friends Church in Yorba Linda, California. Adapted from Dr. Mylander's book **SECRETS OF GROWING CHURCHES** (Harper & Row, 1979). Used by permission.

What builds morale in your church? How do leaders set a climate of excitement and expectancy? What ingredients go into an effective mix of *esprit de corps*? Definite patterns emerge in high morale, growing churches...

Morale builds through a contagious sense of expectancy. In growing churches high expectations flow between people and pastor. The people hold a remarkable sense of confidence in their minister. They like him as a person and in his role as "our pastor." They follow his philosophy of ministry with enthusiasm. Over a period of time they give their minister authority to correspond to his responsibility. As he proves his God-given leadership, they give him the power to make crucial decisions. They expect him to lead the church.

A successful pastor seldom gains such confidence from his people in less than five years. Satisfying relationships result from weeks, months, and years of faithfulness.

In high morale churches the interaction between people and pastor sets the tone as positive, helpful, supportive. The pastor is affirming of his people and their gifts, of the church and its great possibilities and opportunities. The people are supportive of their pastor, willing to give generously of their time and energy, and rally behind his leadership. There is a beautiful spirit of trust, of giving, of love between pastor and people in a high morale church. It reminds me of the tale of the little village in an isolated land where the people shared a boundless sense of happiness. A careful examination showed only one unusual feature about their life together. They engaged in a delightful custom of giving fuzzies to each other. Something about fuzzies felt good and made people happy.

Then one day someone became upset over something petty and started a nasty rumor of retaliation. "Have you heard about the coming shortage of fuzzies?" the disgruntled member of the community began asking. Before long the people began hiding their fuzzies. They buried them in fields, hid them in out-of-the-way places, locked them in vaults. Only on birthdays or anniversaries did they wrap up fuzzies as special presents. In time they quit giving them altogether.

As you might expect, the little village developed into a miserable place to live. People became sad, gloomy, depressed. Discord and strife broke out. Tension and suspicion replaced the former trust and confidence.

Then, one day while some of the children were playing in a field, they stumbled onto a hidden cache of fuzzies. The tingle to their touch felt wonderful. With delighted laughter they gave some to their friends. The more they gave them away, the happier they felt. The adults soon noticed and remembered the old days.

Soon they too joined the fun and brought out their fuzzies from hiding. And, as you might expect, the village became an uplifting place to live again. What are fuzzies? Nothing more than heartfelt compliments and sincere appreciation. Not flattery, true fuzzies build up another person's morale. The legend illustrates what can happen between people and pastor in a local congregation.

High morale builds in a church through a sense of expectancy in both programming and problem-solving. While the methods vary, the constant is that pastors and lay leaders in high morale churches generate excitement for the church program. The leadership keeps communicating that something good is happening and is going to continue to happen. Intangible feelings like joy, anticipation, and achievement soon became the prevailing norm.

Most of the attention in a growing church focuses on Christ rather than on problems. Morale builds through a contagious sense of expectancy toward God. Members really believe in Christ's presence among them in the concrete reality of a personal encounter. Their attitude in approaching worship radiates an electric expectancy, "God is here right now." The people anticipate the Lord's touch to heal personal hurts and grant Christ's forgiveness.

Christians in growing churches share a deep-seated enthusiasm about Jesus Christ. By telling of their own experiences in receiving Christ, the members give one another permission to speak of spiritual things. God's supernatural working slips into casual conversations, especially when the topic turns to a personal crisis or the need for guidance. Answered prayer and new insights from the Bible cause as much excitement as a recent job promotion or a new baby.

An intense belief about the gospel's life-changing power permeates growing churches. The congregation reads about the gospel in Scripture and then experiences it in everyday life. They feel convinced that life is better now and for all eternity because of a receptive response to the Biblical message. As a result they want their friends to find the same kind of help. As the old saying puts it, "Nothing beats a satisfied customer."

A contagious sense of expectancy helps a church grow. But it cannot be maintained without a repeated pattern of satisfying experiences. Blind faith may start a man down a promising path. But if he stumbles again and again, his hopes and dreams will soon evaporate. But if step after step gives him steady progress forward, he expects more.

Mark it down as a principle. Morale builds through a series of good experiences. What will help a church forge a better set of experiences for its people?

A deep level of trust sets the foundation. As a moral value, trust is on the wane today, and suspicion moves in wherever integrity is lost. Distrust runs rampant in politics, education and business. The present moral decline eroding Christian values in the Western world presents grave consequences. The stability of the economy, strength of the family and survival of basic freedoms stand in jeopardy.

The sense of mutual confidence within the church must stand in stark contrast to the outside world for morale to increase. No other institution on earth holds so great a basis for authentic trust. It emerges from the very nature and mighty acts of triune God.

Finances, perhaps more than any other objective indicator, reveal a church's level of unselfishness. I measured "external giving" in four growing churches for my doctoral dissertation. External giving includes all the money the church gives outside of itself for such items as missions, community outreach, benevolences and denominational assessments. Internal giving, in contrast, reflects what the local church spends to maintain itself, such as salaries, buildings, and supplies. The external giving for these four growing churches averaged quite high, 25% of their total income.

Another doctoral study of five growing churches, ranging in size from two hundred to two thousand, also investigated external and internal giving. The five averaged 19% in external giving, far more than most churches. Per capita giving, too, in all the congregations of both studies far exceeded denominational averages. Growing churches care about God's work in the world and express it in tangible terms. Their sacrifice calls for more volunteer labor and scrutinized budgets. Yet God honors their faith through the by-product of high morale. The correlation between church growth and unselfishness is significant.

Contagious expectancy and good experiences both contribute to high morale. Expectancy builds positive feelings and good experiences enhance warm relationships. Yet the two will not do by themselves. Something of God must show in what the church accomplishes. One more characteristic calls for attention.

Morale builds through God-given achievement. Visit any fast-growing church and see for yourself. Watch the smiles light up on the people's faces as you ask the simple question, "How are things going at your church?" Then step back and listen to an enthusiastic report of God's accomplishments in their midst.

With steady growth the congregation senses the vitality of their church. Their inner discernment is no illusion since both the organism and the organization are growing.

Someone may ask which comes first, the chicken or the egg? Does high morale produce growth or does a growing church build extraordinary morale? Each affects the other in an upward spiral. However, it will prove more productive to place the stress on morale first. With careful attention a spirit of joy will become the normal feeling-tone of the congregation. Such a healthy spiritual climate stimulates attention to growth. A church with low morale, on the other hand, finds growth efforts difficult and discouraging.

Measurable progress toward the church's "owned" goals elevates morale. Church leaders demonstrate that they own a goal by taking action. A growth goal, for example, might require added space and parking, another evangelism staff member or second worship service. It might require more Sunday school classes and fellowship groups to incorporate the new people. The church owns the goal only when it expends the time, money, energy, and prayer to add the increments which make continuous growth possible.

Goal achievement serves as such an integral part of high morale that Ralph R. Bentley and Averno M. Rempel of Purdue University build it into their definition of the term. They define morale as "the interest and enthusiasm that a person displays toward the achievement of individual and group goals in a given situation." Note that both individual and group goals need attainment. A growing church embraces a series of interacting objectives. The members of a growing church strive together for common goals which reflect many individual desires. Everyone active in the church feels one or two of his own dreams is finding fulfillment.

Genuine achievement means a high degree of spiritual health. My own research confirmed what other church growth investigators found previously: churches with a high evaluation of spiritual health are sustaining rapid growth rates. When a church considers itself quite healthy, yet shows little interest in growth, the prognosis for such a tragic attitude is only decline and decay.

Morale builds through contagious expectancy, good experiences, and God-given achievement. A climate of high morale creates optimum conditions for church growth, and church growth, in its basic form, is fulfillment of our Lord's central purpose and desire for His church.

Three Characteristics of a Successful Pastor

BY DR. ROBERT SCHULLER

Almost without exception, the successful pastor is first of all an effective leader. And in nearly every unsuccessful situation, the reason is lack of leadership. So one major question concerning the pastor and church growth is: "what is leadership?"

Real leadership is the quality that defines the *role*, sets the *goal*, then pays the *toll!*

First, what is the pastor's role? His role, very simply, is to lead—to think ahead, to plan for the future, to search for all possibilities, to envision problems and dream up solutions, and then to communicate these possibilities and problem-solving ideas to the church decision-makers. The successful pastor is always thinking ahead of everyone else. He can't live in the past. He must live in the future. Effective leadership draws its inspiration from future projections, not from past accomplishments. The successful pastor must also define the role of the church. I define the role in our church as the body of Christ in the community, looking for people who are hurting, loving them and lifting them to an experience of the redeeming grace of God.

Dr. Schuller is senior pastor of the Garden Grove Community Church, Garden Grove, California.

The successful church ministers to totality of human relationships and needs in its community.

I can think of some churches that are simply preaching stations—they have great crowds on Sunday morning, but little, if anything, else going on to meet human needs. Then there are the training center or evangelism center churches. But the great church of today must be more than these. The successful church will always be the body of Christ, reaching out to hurting people through evangelism, education, training, ministry-worship, and meeting the unique needs of its people.

Second, the successful pastor sets the goals for the church. Now this requires that the pastor stay in a church long enough to know his people, the community and their needs. In too many churches, the minister comes with the idea that he will stay until something better comes along. That is a guaranteed formula...for failure. *Bloom where you are planted!* Success is not a matter of latitude, but the direct result of attitude. Great movements are never attracted to great places, but are always attracted to great ideas. And successful ideas always move from a beautiful inspiring dream to *specific measurable goals.*

So how do you set goals? You begin by making a list of the greatest *needs* in your church and in your community. Then prioritize your list. What is the most pressing need? What can you do *now*? Based on these needs, set clear, specific and definable goals that describe the *results* you project one year from now, five years, and ten years.

Then test your goals. I use three questions to determine whether my goals are inspired by God. First, is this a problem-solving goal? Will the achievement of this goal—this dream—solve human problems? If the answer is yes, I'm ready for the next question: Is this dream—my inspired goal—pacesetting? Or is someone else already successfully meeting these needs? If your goal is pacesetting, you can be assured of exciting new challenges and opportunities, and the people whose problems will be solved by your goal will know you are in God's business. If your goal passes these two tests, then you ask the greatest question: Will this bring glory to God? Will it be a great thing for God? And if you have answered "yes" to all three questions, then it's time to get started, for beginning is half done! And that's the third point—*the successful pastor is willing to pay the toll in order to get the job done*. In setting your goals, believe that anything is possible if it can solve human problems and if it can be a great thing for God. See the possibilities and then set your goals. Dream up all of the possible ways to reach your goal. And then dig in and work! Pay the toll!

Mass Evangelism: The Bottom Line

BY DR. WIN ARN

What Christian hasn't thrilled to the moment of invitation at a Billy Graham Crusade?

Via television or in person, hearts beat faster...spiritual temperatures rise... "Just As I am" resonates through the auditorium...and people by the scores begin walking down the aisle.

Preceding this moment have been months, even years of preparation. Committees have been formed, offices rented, churches recruited, budgets raised, counselors trained, prayers offered, publicity distributed...everything in anticipation of that final moment of truth.

For over 20 years the standard for mass evangelism has been set by the Billy Graham Crusades. Graham himself is a national institution—unquestionably the best known and respected spokesman of Christianity in America. His name consistently appears as one of America's 10 most respected men. Most Christians, including myself, hold him in high esteem.

The quest of this paper is evaluation and improvement of a method—not a man. The goal is to improve a good

Win Arn, President and Executive Director of the Institute For American Church Growth, is one of the leading authors, film producers, authorities in the field of Church Growth.

method's effectiveness as it contributes to the actual growth of the Body of Christ...the local church. It is our firm conviction that God will use effective evangelism to make His Church grow. Visible, countable, substantial numbers of people will be added to the Church. The book of Acts records again and again that those who believed were added to the Church—the existing fellowship of Christians. Today, as a result of our mass evangelistic endeavors, are believers still added to existing fellowships?

When the crowds are gone, and the evangelistic crusades are but a memory—what is the bottom line?

What about the decisions? Are those who respond pagans from the "world" becoming Christians? Or are they already church members coming forward for rededication? Are the decisions incorporated into churches? Are they nurtured into discipleship? Do cooperating churches grow following crusades? How do pastors evaluate evangelism crusades one year later? What *is* the bottom line for mass evangelism?

Surprisingly little research or hard data is available. Mass evangelism crusades are traditionally reported and acclaimed successful by the number in attendance and the number of decisions recorded. Yet, as those who respond to the invitation file into a counseling room, a curtain seems to descend, obliterating the scene...blanketing these decisions in an obscure fog, until the same drama is repeated the next night and the next until the crusade ends. The team leaves town, final mopping up operations are completed, decision cards are referred, and mass evangelism in that city is often laid to rest until another time, perhaps a decade away, when a crusade is again scheduled.

As you read this article on mass evangelism you should know that my own ministry has deep roots in crusade evangelism. For 14 years I personally led an organization where weekly rallies concluded with the appeal for a "decision." I have attended and participated in many evangelistic crusades, including serving as vice chairman of a Billy Graham Crusade as well as chairman of the nominating committee. I am aware that there are many benefits in mass evangelism which cannot be measured and quantitatively determined. Yet from my own experience and background I have come to recognize a crucial principle of effective evangelism.

That principle: *Abundant and accurate information, scientifically gathered, truthfully presented and analyzed, enables Christians to be good stewards of the grace of God and more effective communicators of the Gospel of Jesus Christ.*

Fact gathering and fact analysis helps remove the "fog" which so often obscures reality. Only as abundant information becomes available can Christians honestly evaluate past effectiveness and develop plans and strategies for the future which God can bless to the mighty multiplication of His Church.

This principle is helping to make evangelism more effective. It was recently applied to Campus Crusade's *Here's Life, America,* which was heralded as "the greatest spiritual harvest in the history of the church...100 times, yes 1000 times greater than anything I have ever read about in the almost 2000-year-old history of the church." The bottom line, however, proved the "I Found It" campaign to be ineffective evangelism for making disciples and responsible church members.

Research conducted by The Institute for American Church Growth clearly indicated that of the hundreds of thousands of "decisions" from the Here's Life emphasis, 97 out of every 100 were never incorporated into a church. This pioneering research was followed by a second study by the Fuller Evangelistic Association under the sponsorship of Campus Crusade. Where there was overlapping, the two surveys were remarkably similar (*Eternity,* Sept. 1977). These research studies helped convince Crusade leaders to search for more effective ways to be good communicators of the gospel of Jesus Christ. More effective evangelism is always the end to be sought.

A basic conviction of the church growth movement is that effective evangelism produces measurable results—people discipled and added to the Church. The church growth definition of evangelism is "to proclaim Jesus Christ as God and Savior, to persuade people to become His disciples and responsible members of the Church."

A "decision" is an inadequate concept; a truth recognized by the best evangelists themselves. Leighton Ford recently stated, "if we are true to Jesus' pattern, evangelism will not end with a decision for Christ. The end product of evangelism is not a 'decision' but a mature, growing disciple who is able to reproduce and share Christ with others" (Eternity, Sept. 1977). True…but effective evangelism is not only making disciples, it is actively incorporating converts into the Body—the Church—where they function as responsible members.

If making disciples and incorporating them into the Body is the bottom line for effective evangelism, what results are produced by mass evangelistic crusades?

Many different evangelistic campaigns could have been chosen; however, because the Greater Seattle Crusade was apparently so successful, research was conducted one year later by Church Growth: America magazine. Decision magazine (Aug. 76) described that crusade as "…most exciting and successful U.S. Billy Graham crusade in years." Under the banner "Rescue for Seattle," Decision reported that a total of 434,100 persons had passed through the gate…and of that number 18,136 walked down onto the astroturf or stood in place…" "5700 persons had completed the studies and qualified as counselors. The figure exceeded that of any other crusade in the Graham's team history."

One year later, to what extent had Seattle been rescued?

To find the answer a questionnaire was sent to 1200 pastors in the Greater Seattle/Tacoma Area. The following questions were asked, with responses tabulated below:

QUESTION: Did your church cooperate in the Billy Graham Crusade?

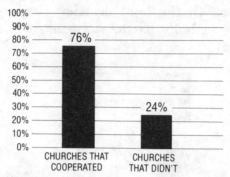

COMMENT: The proportion of participating churches, when compared to the number who participated in the *Here's Life America* blitz, is much higher. (Approximately 30% of the churches in a community participated in *Here's Life*). Graham's mass evangelism seems to have a much broader base of support.

QUESTION: Of the follow-up cards your church received, how many were for Conversion? Rededication? Unknown?

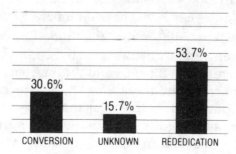

COMMENT: The results of this particular crusade appear to have made a more substantial impact on the Christian community than on the non-Christian community. With over half of those who respond already claiming to be Christians (53.7%), and another 15.7% uncertain as to why they responded, might mass evangelism in this and many other cases be more accurately termed "mass revival?"

QUESTION: Of the total decision cards you received, how many actually participated in the nurture groups? Completed?

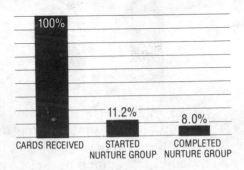

CARDS RECEIVED · STARTED NURTURE GROUP · COMPLETED NURTURE GROUP

COMMENT: The nurture group (a crusade-sponsored post-decision follow up) was only partially effective following this crusade. 89 of every 100 who responded to the invitation never became involved. However, of those 11 involved, 8 eventually completed the class.

QUESTION: As a direct result of the crusade, how many are now (one year later) new members of your church?

COMMENT: Assuming that the "rededication" decisions (53.7%) were already members of the church, then from the total "conversion" (30.6%) and "unknown" (15.7%) decision cards received, the above 15.3% are now in a local church. Compared to the total number of decisions, the figure drops to slightly over 7%. On the surface one must lament the great loss to the Body of those who respond but are not incorporated. The figure of 15% incorporation is difficult to make an abritrary judgment on. But certainly 85 out of every 100 professing conversions now not incorporated in a church does leave room for concern. More research is needed on "the fruit which remains."

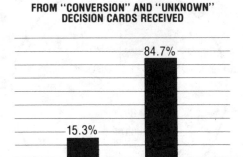

FROM "CONVERSION" AND "UNKNOWN"
DECISION CARDS RECEIVED

QUESTION: Of the total decisions sent to your church, how many were already attending or associated with your church?

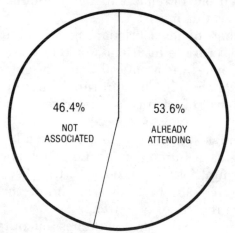

COMMENT: This figure (53.6%) corresponds almost exactly with the number of people who came forward for "rededication"—again indicating the crusade's revival/renewal aspects.

QUESTION: How many of those new members were friends or relatives of people already in your church?

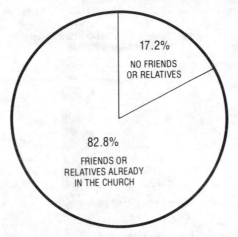

17.2%

NO FRIENDS
OR RELATIVES

82.8%

FRIENDS OR
RELATIVES ALREADY
IN THE CHURCH

COMMENT: Here's a "gold mine" discovery! Of the 15% crusade conversions now in a church, over 8 out of every 10 already had a friend or relative in that particular congregation. What does this mean?

Large numbers of new Christians now in churches were invited to the crusade by friends or relatives. Following the decision there was a natural "door of entrance" into that same local church. This built-in follow-up, using established "webs" of friends and relatives, is particularly effective.

These findings support previous research by The Institute for American Church Growth. Over 8000 people in 35 states and 3 countries were asked why they became part of a local church. 75% to 90% responded that friends/relatives were the "door of entrance."

The conclusion is clear...churches encouraging and equipping their members to reach the existing webs of friends and relatives, and then building them into the fellowship of the local church, will experience greatest results for their time and effort.

QUESTION: Would you, as pastor, be in favor of another crusade in the next 3 years?

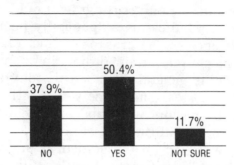

COMMENT: This question was asked primarily for interest's sake and should not be associated with any significant attitude change, since it is unknown what feelings were prior to the crusade.

QUESTION: One year later, what are your feelings about the crusade's relationship to the growth of your church?

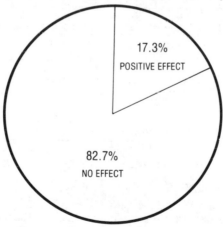

COMMENT: This was an open-ended question for the pastor to complete himself. Comments by pastors were, however, categorized by our staff into "generally positive effect" and "no effect" on the growth of their church.

It was interesting to note that of *all* the cards received, not one pastor commented that the crusade had had a positive effect on the *numerical growth* of his church. All of the responses indicating a "generally positive effect" were in reference to the crusade's effect on the people already in the church ("trained them in counseling, sharing faith") or its general effect on the city ("raised the God-consciousness"). The perceived positive impact of the crusade by pastors was substantially in the area of renewal and/or visibility.

In overview, based on the statistical projection of responses received, the Greater Seattle Billy Graham Crusade appears as follows:

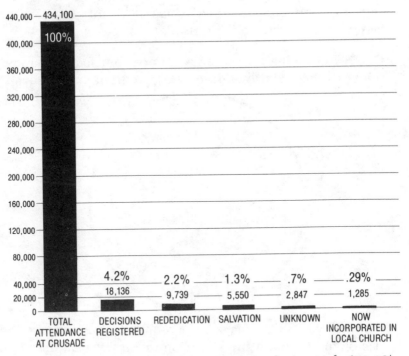

Based on the analysis of decisions in the crusade (53.7% Rededication, 30.6% Conversion and 15.7% Unknown), and the number of presently incorporated "conversion" decisions, a projected total for the final results of the Seattle crusade look like this:

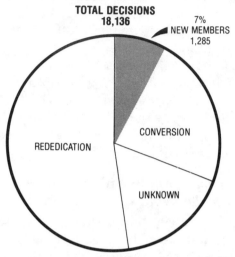

TOTAL DECISIONS 18,136

7% NEW MEMBERS 1,285

REDEDICATION

CONVERSION

UNKNOWN

A NEW STRATEGY FOR MASS EVANGELISM

Can the "method" of mass evangelism be more effective in reaching people for Jesus Christ and incorporating them into His Body? Yes and no. Apparently not, if we continue doing it the same old way. There is nothing sacred about methods. Because "we've always done it that way" is no guarantee we should continue doing it that way. The acid test: do the methods produce the results desired? If so, continue. If not, methods should be adjusted, modified, or reconsidered.

The following steps are suggested for more effective mass evangelism, when conducted by churches, evangelist or ministers:

1. Change the goal from registering decisions to "making disciples and responsible members of the church."

This change of emphasis structured into crusade evangelism will sharpen the purpose, deepen the concept, strengthen the results, and provide a solid basis for evaluation. It is not enough to simply wish that "decisions" become established in a church...effective evangelism demands that the goal of making disciples and incorporating in the Body be a major platform of every mass-evangelism crusade.

A higher level of "God-consciousness" and rededicated Christians following a crusade, while excellent, is not and should not be the measure of success. The "bottom line" is the actual, factual growth of the Body through new Christians beginning a life-changing experience as responsible church members in a local congregation.

2. *Precede each crusade with adequate church growth training for pastors and key lay leaders.*

A magnificent contribution of mass evangelism to cooperating churches could be the training of pastors/laity in church growth principles and practical applications. Such a foundation would literally transform the churches as they built evangelism/growth principles into the very fiber of their existence. New insights, research, principles, practices in church growth are being significantly blessed of God worldwide to the multiplication of the Church. Seminars and training could add a significant and much needed new dimension to mass evangelism. An early step in preparation for an evangelistic crusade would be for cooperating churches to study church growth and set growth goals, including new members in existing churches as well as establishing new branch churches in unreached pockets of society.

A preliminary model for combining church growth concepts and mass evangelism had its first test recently. Called the "Rosario Plan," church growth training preceded, by 15 months, a crusade conducted by Louis Palau in South America. One significant innovation in the plan was to properly locate the evangelistic event within the total growth process. Instead of simply planning a crusade and hoping churches grew as a result, concentration was on building a "growth dynamic" within co-operating churches long before the crusade took place. Because of this training, when the crusade began there were already 42 new churches established, and congregations were much more prepared to incorporate new converts. More thinking and planning is needed both in the United States and worldwide for structuring church growth principles into an integral part of mass evangelistic endeavors.

3. Elevate the importance of the local church in mass-evangelism.

There presently exists a "gap" between the glamour of the crusade, with the testimonies of super-stars and 5000 voice choir, and the local pastors, backed by the 15 voice choir. A person born in the excitement, glamour, crowds, starlets and media of a crusade often finds the local church flat, dull, and boring.

Established Christians and new converts need to know that the real "action" takes place not at the crusade, but in and through the local church. This concept must be incorporated in a fresh way into mass evangelism. Research indicates that the greater the gap between the local church and the evangelistic effort, the less "fruit" will remain.

4. Encourage and train laity to evangelize.

A crusade is often like a large football game with thousands of spectators cheering their team forward, watching a few players on the field trying to advance the ball. When spectators become participants, it becomes a whole new ball game.

The emphasis must shift from platform to pew; from clergy to laity. Effective evangelism in a community takes place when those who live there, alive in Christ, share the miracle of salvation with their friends, neighbors, and relatives. This sharing takes place not inside the walls of a stadium, or even a church, but outside—on the job, in the home, in the school—in the arena of life. Throughout history the Church has surged forward as laity have taken the good news into every corner of their world.

In the Seattle crusade 5,700 were trained as counselors to help anyone who came forward. What might have happened if those same people, or perhaps twice that number, had been trained to effectively communicate Christ in their sphere of influence, to present their faith to their friends, and bring these people into their churches? And what if they had used their training faithfully for 12 months? With such a plan Seattle might have indeed been "rescued." Effective evangelism must always involve the laity...involvement which enables, trains, and supports great numbers of laity sharing the good news in Christ throughout the vast mosaics which make up every community. This church growth principle can and must become part of mass evangelism. Perhaps Billy Graham could be entering his period of greatest influence by incorporating such a training of laity into his crusades.

5. Develop and utilize natural bridges of evangelism through friends and relations.

Research of the Seattle crusade revealed that 83% of those who, one year later, are now incorporated into the church, had friends or relatives already in that church! What an important clue for effective evangelism.

Carrying the Gospel across these natural bridges is a strategy which has abundant blessing of God. By utilizing these "bridges," crusade evangelism would increase its effectiveness many times over...and the new converts would be incorporated!

6. Structure a year-round strategy of effective evangelism in participating local churches.

Obedience to the Great Commission takes place when each congregation builds into its structure effective evangelism which functions day by day, week by week, month by month, year by year. When that happens, so does this: "...and the Lord added to the Church daily such of those who were being saved."

When a year-round strategy for evangelism is applied in local congregations, the mass evangelistic effort is not a once-a-decade end in itself, but part of a greater strategy providing a unique resource which local churches can use as a part of their greater plan. Then the churches do not serve the crusade...but the crusade becomes the servant of the churches.

What might be the results of implementing these six steps into campaigns of mass evangelism?

A new outpouring of God's grace and power in the world through His Church!

When the next mass evangelistic crusade is planned for your city, we suggest you and your church build in these ideas, for as we begin developing church growth eyes and seeing new possibilities, as we discover ways that prove effective and discard ways that are ineffective, we will find ourselves in a new age of vitality. With God's blessing and the indwelling of the Holy Spirit, we are going to see the Church making great advances throughout the world! The fact is that multitudes of winnable people are waiting to be won. As we refine our methods and develop effective strategies, churches will receive the abundant blessing God wants to give.

The Biblical Pattern of Effective Evangelism

BY TOM WOLF

The motto of many churches for evangelism has become: doing it more but enjoying it less. Eyes roll when the bus ministry is mentioned, fear seizes the stomach when door-to-door visitation is hinted at, and general apathy reigns over attempts to involve members in another exciting, dynamic, lifechanging, $23 weekend witnessing clinic.

Why is it that in the New Testament outreach seems so much fun, so vibrant and natural, while today's evangelism often suits out as forced, dutiful and (to the laymen if not the officials) unnatural?

Perhaps some of the answer lies in the fact that we all have no trouble understanding Paul's clear precedent when he says, "I did not shrink from teaching you publicly and from house to house" (Acts 20:20). But we are left somewhat mystified by the Lord Jesus when he exhorts us, "Do not go from house to house" (Luke 10:7). Why, everyone knows that Paul set in motion the time-tested tradition of going door to door in "cold turkey" prospect evangelism. Didn't he? And then, of course, whatever Jesus meant in Luke, well, it probably doesn't apply to us today because of a different dispensational context. Right?

Rev. Wolf is senior pastor of The Church on Brady in Los Angeles.

Several fundamental insights from contemporary anthropology help us understand more clearly the biblical pattern of evangelism which flowed so freely, fearlessly and forcefully through the early church across the Mediterranean world.

Peter B. Hammond, Professor of Anthropology at Indiana University, observes that "in most cultures the social systems of greatest importance are based on kinship. Human beings everywhere are born into some sort of family. And almost always this family is important in giving them—literally and figuratively—a start in life: producing them, feeding, clothing, protecting, and educating them, and eventually establishing for them a 'place' in society...In most cultures the kin group plays an even more important role [than in America], lasting throughout life as the principal source of the individual's emotional, economic, social—and frequently supernatural—support, and providing the basis for community organization."[1]

David G. Mandelbaum, Professor of Anthropology, University of California, summarizes his findings: "Whatever diversity there may be among social groupings the world over, there are at least two types which are found in every human society. The family is one of them...In every land, among every people, the child is ordinarily raised and nurtured within a family. The other type of group universal to humanity...is the local community. Just as no person normally lives all his life alone, devoid of any family, so does no family normally live entirely alone, apart from any local group...of neighbors."[2]

Mandelbaum goes on to point out a third group—the clan—which is also a cultural universal, if one allows for its evolution in the contemporary Western setting. The clan has developed into "...the social units which are extensions of the local group...voluntary associations based on common interests...ranging from trade unions and medical associations to bridge clubs and parent-teacher associations. Each of these groupings is held together by a common interest, an interest arising from mutual participation in the same trades, the mutual enjoyment of a game, or mutual problems in relation to a set of children."[3]

The three universal units of societies worldwide, according to anthropological research, are social systems based on 1) common kinship, 2) common community, and 3) common interests. Now let us go one step further. Since this triunity of social systems is a part of present day human life, would we be so surprised to discover the same central characteristics in the human matrix of social life in the times of the New Testament? In fact, that is exactly what we find. For this phenomenon is not only transcultural, it is transhistorical, reaching across centuries.

The apostolic church used the interlocking social systems of common kinship/community/interests as the backbone for communicating the Gospel. The basic thrust of New Testament evangelism was not individual evangelism, it was not mass evangelism, and it was definitely not child evangelism. The normative pattern of evangelism in the early church was *oikos evangelism.*

"Oikos Evangelism." What is it? *Oikos* is the Greek word most often translated *house* or *household* evangelism. But be careful. Don't just assume you know what those words mean. Of course we know their basic meaning in English. But what was their original connotation?

Under the old Attic law, *oikos* was *the whole estate,* while *oikia* was the *physical dwelling* only. However, that precise distinction was lost in later Greek. In the New Testament there are several places where *oikia* actually means the *inhabitants of a house* (Mt. 12:25; Jn. 4:53; I Cor. 16:15; Phil. 4:22).

Oikos means *a house.* Specifically, it means an *inhabited* house in contrast to *domos,* the mere building itself. Thus, one can understand the significance of a house being a dwelling. Oikos was sometimes used to specify a certain kind of inhabited building such as a temple, a palace, or even a grave.

It was common in Egypt to call a temple the oikos of the deity. The papyri refer to "the oikos of Ammon" in the main temple of Hephaestus. The anthropological literature records the basic animistic practice of consecrating an image or shrine to a spirit and inviting the spirit to come and indwell the shrine. Such is the significance of Micah's oikos/shrine for the spirits during the times of the Judges (Judges 17:5).

The oikos of the Lord of Israel was the chosen place for His presence (Judges 18:31; II Sam. 12:20), though there was continual clarification that the Lord of all the earth does not dwell in buildings made by man (Is. 66:1–2; I Kings 8:12–21, 27–30; Jer. 7:1–11; Acts 7:46–50).

Jesus spoke of His Father's oikos, sometimes meaning the earthly temple (Jn. 2:16) and sometimes the heavenly dwelling (Jn. 14:2). Spiritually, the body becomes the real oikos/dwelling place of God (I Cor. 3:16; II Cor. 6:16). Even demons will claim men's bodies as an oikos to inhabit when conditions are appropriate (Mt. 12:44; Lk. 11:24) I Timothy 3:15 makes it clear that the Oikos of God "is the church of the living God, the pillar and support of the truth."

In a broader sense, oikos referred to one's entire estate, people and property forming one family, a household, as the usage of oikos applied to the Church would imply. In Israel, the oikos included not only wife and children, but also servants and resident aliens. Thus the command of Deuteronomy 12:7, "You shall eat before the Lord your God, and you shall rejoice, you and your household," is explained by 12:12, "You shall rejoice before the Lord your God, you and your sons and daughters, your menservants and your maidservants." (See also Deut. 14:26.)

This same concept of oikos was just as basic in Graeco-

Roman society and thought. Acts 10 has a casually given, though faithful, definition of oikos. It says that "Cornelius feared God with all his oikos/household" (10:2). An angel of God instructed Cornelius to send for Peter, saying "He will declare to you a message by which you will be saved, you and all your oikos" (11:14). When Peter arrived, "Cornelius was expecting them and had called together his kinsmen and close friends...many persons" (10:24,27). *An oikos is a social system composed of those related to each other through common ties and tasks.* The New Testament oikos included members of the nuclear family, but extended to dependents, slaves and employees. Oikos members often lived together, but always sensed a close association with each other. And, note this carefully, the oikos constituted the basic social unit by which the early church grew, spreading the Good News of Jesus Christ, the risen Lord.

Michael Green *(Evangelism in the Early Church)* confirms that "the [oikos] family understood in this broad way, as consisting of blood relations, slaves, clients, and friends, was one of the bastions of Graeco-Roman society. Christian missionaries made a deliberate point of gaining whatever households they could as lighthouses, so to speak, from which the gospel could illuminate the surrounding darkness...[We are, then,] quite right in stressing the centrality of the [oikos] household to Christian advance."[4]

By thus cleaning the lenses of our socio-historical spectacles, we can see what an oikos meant to the early church. An oikos was the fundamental and natural unit of society, and consisted of one's sphere of influence—his family, friends and associates. And equally important, the early church spread through oikoses—circles of influence and association. With only a moment of reflection, we begin to realize a significant difference of thrust, tone, and tenor between much contemporary evangelism and early church outreach.

The first church does not appear to have had a fanfare of mass campaigns for evangelism. They would have considered it foolishness to organize camel caravans for growth, bringing kids to Timothy's Children's Church with the promise of Bythinia Burgers after the services. (Tell me, now, can you honestly imagine Silas and Titus as camel captains vying for the grand prize going to the camel team averaging the most children at the 1st Ecclesia of Ephesus??) But, joy of joys, the early church was not encumbered with the wholly unnatural (unnatural then and unnatural now) experience of forced evangelism: going reluctantly, flinchingly and embarrassingly door to door to encounter people they did not know, to explain a message which the first time often did not make sense, to an audience totally uninterested or unfriendly.

As Michael Green reminds us, an oikos for the New Testament church consisted of "blood relations, slaves, clients, and friends. Christian missionaries made a deliberate point of gaining whatever [oikos] households they could as lighthouses, so to speak, from which the gospel could illuminate the surrounding darkness." An oikos corresponds to what contemporary anthropologists define as the three universal social systems of common kinship, common community, and common interests.

Oikos evangelism is the God-given and God-ordained means for naturally sharing our supernatural message. The early church spread through oikos evangelism—evangelizing family members who saw the old sinner become the new saint; sharing with the neighbor who questioned how such a difference had come over his old friend; and reaching the guys in the local trade union or the oikos that played tennis together.

It is here, also, that we catch an eye-burning hint of the key to oikos evangelism: life transformation. *If oikos evangelism is God's key to the natural and rapid spread of the Good News, then life transformation is the key to oikos penetration and persuasion.* Life transformation. Maybe that. is why some adults are forced into evangelizing only children. Could it be that the children do not yet see what the adult peer groups so clearly perceive—that one has become religious without becoming radiant? And could this also be a clue to why, all too often, the persons who are so gung-ho on doorbell evangelism seem...er, uh, well, not to offend anyone, they just seem a little strange? Now, don't get me wrong. They are sincere; unquestionably so. And they are enthusiastic; embarrassingly so. And yet, so help me, I've met a lot of them, and well... Could it be that some of us in the contemporary church who are so bold to evangelize "out there" fall fruitless "right here" in our own oikos? In the early church, it was the restoration of balance, the restitution of wrongs, and the fragrance of an enchanting new life that drew so many to the fledgling oikos of God.

"Believe on the Lord Jesus Christ and you shall be saved, you and your oikos." (Acts 16:31) That is the apostolic answer to the question, "What must I do to be saved?" The spread of the faith is included in the reception of the faith. Oikos evangelism is God's natural means to spread the Good News, for everyone who has ever, or will ever, receive Christ. And the key that opens every oikos is life transformation through the indwelling of the living God.

FOOTNOTES

1. Hammond, Peter. *Cultural & Social Anthropology: Selected Readings.* 1964: 145–46. MacMillan: New York.
2. Mandelbaum, David. "Social Groupings" in Hammond (ed) *Cultural & Social Anthropology.* (see above).
3. Ibid.
4. Green, Michael. *Evangelism in The Early Church,* 1970: 210 Eerdmans: Grand Rapids. (For additional comments see pp. 207–223.)

A Strategy for Media BY RUSS REID and Your Church

**A Leading Advertising Executive Shares
Insights to Help You Promote Your
Church's Ministry in Your Community.**

*The Pasadena Advanced Growth Seminar for
Professionals presents a unique variety of expertise in
the various areas of church growth. The following
article, by Russ Reid, is part of a lecture presented at a
recent Advanced Seminar.*

I remember years ago when I was asked to speak at a
special gathering of pastors, the man responsible to introduce me was very uncomfortable. He finally blurted out,
"Mr. Reid, is there any other way I could introduce you
besides president of an advertising agency?" I smiled and
told him "No, that is what I am."

As I reflected on that after the meeting, I think I understood some of the reservations he had about an ad agency
in its normal context. There's a lot about Madison Avenue
that isn't really very good. You know, we're told that if you
want to get over boredom you buy a Mustang, if you want
to have a good time you drink Budweiser, and if your day is

Mr. Russ Reid is president of one of the major Christian advertising
agencies in the country.

tumbling in, the best solution is to watch the Mike Douglas show. The thing advertising agencies have done here is really very strategic. They've spent millions of dollars in research identifying human needs, but they're offering bromides for those human needs instead of real solutions. The tragic thing is that we in the church stand by and say isn't it terrible the bad solutions they offer to man's real problems. Yet for the most part we have failed to understand how to communicate to these same troubled people so we can offer them the answer in terms that really do provide solutions.

There are three basic areas I'd like to talk about in terms of communication and the growth of your church. One is public relations, the second is publicity, the third is advertising. There is a certain amount of overlap between these terms, but for our purposes I'd like to keep them separate.

PUBLIC RELATIONS

The definition I use for public relations is: the art of creating an environment where your message will be heard under favorable conditions.

What is good public relations? Let's start there. You know one of the great myths of the PR business is that a PR practitioner can walk into a situation, wave a magic wand and it really doesn't matter what is going on, he can make it look good. Well, unfortunately, or perhaps fortunately, that is not the case. The first thing that has to happen in your church, in creating an environment for your message to be heard, is that something must be going on that's worthwhile. I can't emphasize this enough. You can't build a program on puff if God isn't working in your church and lives aren't being changed.

I remember, years ago, an evangelist of some note came to me. He began painting a scenario of how he saw himself becoming the emerging Billy Graham. The thing he needed was a man like me to put him across! He created absolutely the greatest scenario you ever could hope to see. He'd gotten a post office box with all the same numbers in it, so it would be easy to remember when he announced it over television or radio. And he went right down the line. In fact, he rewrote Billy Graham's story to sound like all the things that happened to Billy Graham were the result of some public relations man's ideas. After he finished I said, "I really think you've misunderstood how God works. I think if you go back to the Old Testament you'll find that Moses was confronted with the burning bush. I think you'll find that Elisha was confronted with the fire. I think you'll find that the Apostle Paul was confronted on the road to Damascus with what was called a conversion experience. And, I think if you read church history you'll find that men God used had a special anointing, a special awakening: it's called by all kinds of theological terms. But one thing it means for sure is that their lives were touched by God." And I said, "When evidence of that happens, so that something is happening in your ministry, then somebody can come along and tell that good news to other people. That really is all public relations is. But until that happens, there isn't a thing in the world I can do for you." We haven't been very good friends since that day.

A good example of successful public relations from the secular world is two automobiles we all are aware of. One is called the Mustang. When the Mustang was introduced in the mid-60s, there was hardly a magazine that did not have a spread on the car. Everybody was talking about the Mustang. The public got to drive it and validated what the PR people were saying. It became the hottest car of the year.

Have you heard of the Edsel? Same amount of money spent; but the car didn't live up to the PR man's story. And it failed. Maybe Abraham Lincoln was right about how many times you can fool the people. We need to get the myth out of the way that you can somehow, with a public relations program, build your church. That's puff and it won't work. It may work for a time, but it will not ultimately build your church. The most important thing you can do is make sure your people are involved in the life of the community and are witnessing and sharing their lives in a way that makes people pay attention to what's going on.

PUBLICITY

Public relations is creating an environment so your message can be accepted in a favorable environment. Publicity, then, is taking, say, an event and promoting it in such a way that people attend. It can be an evangelistic service, a Sunday night service, it can be a prayer group, a Sunday School picnic—it doesn't really matter what it is. But publicity is taking what is going on in your church and giving it public exposure.

Now the first thing you have to do in publicizing something about your church to the community is to publicize what is going on in your church to your own people. You need to create a sense of God at work in your own church—to your own people—before you worry about talking to the community.

A couple of years ago, I was asked if I would be the stewardship director for our church. Now, I don't usually like doing things like that because I do it all week at work. But I said "yes."

One of the first things I decided to do was to interview the staff members of the church. It is a large church, 3000 members, and there are 13 full-time staff. I took my lunch hours every day and interviewed each one. I asked them to tell me what was going on in the church. It was an exciting experience. I discovered it was impossible for one person to know what's going on in the church by just going to Sunday morning service. Through these lunches I became a repository for the exciting information of how God was at work in our church. My job, then, was to communicate God's exciting work to the congregation.

I have a suspicion that when people are asked to give to a church program, they don't give to budgets. They want to see where something is happening in the life of the church; where a man was blind and now he sees. They give to people. Budgets don't translate that. But that's the way our church had been doing it for years. The elders had to go out on Stewardship Sunday with those cards and visit every home and say, "What are you going to do this year?"

So this time we had a banquet, which I suggested the church pay for. We took all the information I had gathered and translated it into a little tabloid. All it said was, "God at work in the church." I gave story after story of what was happening, in marriage counseling, in children's work, in the Day Care Center, in everything that was going on. And then we translated that into an audio-visual presentation. At the banquet we showed it and then took our pledges. Giving went up 35%, because we highlighted God at work in the church. That audio-visual presentation has been retained and is shown now to all new members who come into our church, so they get up to speed on everything that's going on. I think the pastor would say that turned the corner in our church in terms of excitement and enthusiasm for what God was doing.

So before you start any external publicity program, make sure your own people are aware of what's going on and they're turned on by it. Then they will become your best advertisement to help your church grow. After that you have a responsibility to take your story to your community.

There are a number of things we know about local media that can be helpful in church growth. Now, no newspaper is going to publish your church's attendance for the last week. And they probably aren't too interested in who was converted lately. Those aren't stories that have mass appeal to their readers. You have to figure out what it is the editor wants.

Do you realize if you were to pick up the *Los Angeles*

Times, take a red pen and underline everything that was submitted by somebody like me, 80% of the paper would be underlined? Only hard news and editorials are generated internally. And even editorials many times come from public relations people. We're their bread and butter, and so are you. Every editor is looking for good stories. Somebody who will have the imagination to take something going on and write it up in a way that will be interesting to the community. Ask yourself, "What do we have going on in our church that relates to the community?" Do you have a Day Care Center? Do you have a remedial reading program? Do you have a counseling center? Do you have a summer recreational program? Those are programs that tie in to where the community is. It gives you an opportunity to reach people where they are and get them involved in programs where you introduce them to the Savior.

Obviously it is a lot easier to get coverage in the *Pasadena Star-News* than it is in the *Los Angeles Times*. But don't bug the people in the media with trivia. If you only can go down there once a year with a great story, do it once a year. But don't be afraid they don't have time for you, because the editor is looking for good human interest stories and he'll be open to your suggestions. Build a line of communication with him.

ADVERTISING

What about advertising? I once took the *Los Angeles Times*, the *Herald Examiner*, the *San Gabriel News* and the *Pasadena Star-News* and tore out the church pages. I read all the marvelous sermon topics I was invited to go hear. Something like this: "We Hold These Truths," Dr. Jones speaking; "Searching Hearts and Marching Stars," "From Dust to Flesh," "The Light is One," "Interesting Fundamental Bible Teaching"—that'll get 'em every time; "Start the Year with Love and Sound Doctrine." Now those were all from congregations that I would consider evangelical, concerned with making a difference in the lives of people in their community.

Now as an advertising man, I have to ask a couple of questions. Who is the target? Who are they trying to reach with headlines like that? Well, you might say they are trying to get people going to one church to go to another church. That's what we call switching brands in advertising business. We're spending 20 million dollars a year in that kind of newspaper advertising to get people to switch from going to the Presbyterian Church to the Methodist Church. I don't think it works. I actually don't think anybody reads the church page. If I were a pastor I wouldn't spend a dime on that page. At least I wouldn't do it with the kind of advertising that is currently being used.

When I was growing up, Bob Hope used to be sponsored by Pepsodent. Do you remember the slogan—"You'll wonder where the yellow went, when you brush your teeth with Pepsodent." What a promise! What it was really saying was if you use Pepsodent toothpaste, your teeth will be white. They had to build Pepsodent factories all over America because of that ad campaign. The promise was so clear and it was so easy to understand. And I guess it was a true promise because if you used Pepsodent your teeth were white.

What is the promise of the Gospel? Have you ever asked that question? I struggle with it a lot. My theory is that the promise of the Gospel cannot be understood in propositional terms. It can only be understood in relational terms. You see, when I say "Christ is the answer," I really don't have to own that. I can say it, but it doesn't say anything about what Christ has done for me. And it doesn't really tell you how He's the answer, because if you are intelligent at all, you'll say, "Well, what are the questions?" But how many posters have you seen, "Christ is the Answer" or "At the End of the World You'll Meet God"? Propositional. Nobody owns it. The only way you can communicate what Jesus Christ can do in a man's life is by saying, "Once I was blind, now I see." Now there is something that happened to me, and others can identify with that.

You may think from the way I'm talking that I don't believe doctrine is important. It is. We must understand what we believe. But when we're communicating with people who are not a part of the inside group, we need to change our language so they understand what we are talking about. The church page is filled with "in" language that nobody in the world would understand unless they'd been in church since they were toddlers. I don't really think that is what we are trying to do in the church pages ...spend 20 million dollars a year talking to ourselves.

What about a church ad that had a picture of a beautiful woman. The headline said, "When Two Out of Three Are Not Enough" and there were three boxes underneath that said, "Beautiful," Rich," and "Happy." But only "Beautiful" and "Rich" were checked. "Happy" was empty. And the body copy went on to say that there are a lot of people who have wealth but life is still empty. There are a lot of people with beautiful faces who are unhappy. Where does happiness come from?

Now you have to watch out you don't trip up here and say if you become a Christian all of a sudden you will be happy, because that isn't true either. I'll never forget the statement of a preacher I heard in college. He was the pastor of the First Covenant Church in Seattle, Washington. He said, "Jesus Christ did not come to make life easy, but He did come to make you strong." That is the promise of the Gospel. I don't know about your experience as a Christian, but I sure have had my share of trouble. I've had all the problems that I want to have for the rest of my life. But I can tell you, that in the middle of the storm I've had a resource, as a Christian, that helped me overcome these problems and work my way through them, and because of it I am a better person. That's the only promise you can make. If you make any other kind of promise, you're being dishonest. You're being a vacuum cleaner salesman. And I don't think that's what you want to be.

In closing, let me give you a model of what I think would be a good media program for your church. Let me give you just a little bit of marketing background to understand what I'm going to say. If I were a manufacturer of soap and I wanted to introduce a new product, I could hire boys in high school to deliver a package of soap to every house in the community. Or I could put a coupon in the local paper that said, "Ten cents off on this bar of soap at Ralphs." Now if you know anything about economics, you wouldn't use the first for two reasons: one, you can't afford to give away that much soap to people who haven't asked for it. But there is another important reason. The only people you want to give this soap to are people who are asking for it. Those are the only ones, at this particular point in time, who sense a need for a new brand of soap. You are wasting your money by giving it to people who haven't said they want it.

Now what kind of evangelism do many people use in the church today? They give a bar of "soap" to everybody they see, whether they want it or not. We mobilize door-to-door evangelism, we go into communities passing out tracts, ringing door bells. We bother people who don't want to be bothered. And if you're a pastor and you've tried to motivate a group of people to keep that up for very long you know you have a dropout problem that is unbeliev-able. There just aren't many people who can emotionally take "no" ten times out of every eleven they knock on the door.

Now, how does that apply to evangelism in your com-munity? Let's just take a community like Arcadia, Califor-nia. It's a bedroom community for Los Angeles. It doesn't have any industry, and most of the people who live there work somewhere else. It's an upper income community where if you tried knocking at all the doors you'd get in more trouble than you ever bargained for. But in the city of Arcadia, at any given time, there are people who are hurting like crazy. They are going through divorces, they've got problems with their kids, they've got job insecurities, they're worrying about their "Golden Years" when they won't have anything to do. All the pains and hurts of society are in Arcadia, California. And you have a church there.

Well, this is what I would do. I would write a personal letter to everybody in the city of Arcadia. I'd make it a computer letter. Now all that means is that you're able to use personal information on a mass basis and say, "Dear Mr. Johnson, I'm glad I can come into your home today and talk to you about a very personal matter. You may not know me. I'm the pastor of the Arcadia Presbyterian Church. We don't think we've got all the answers where we are, but we do know that we're struggling together to try and find emotional maturity, to try to put our lives together, to try to understand our families, and basically try to figure out how to live in the cockeyed world we're involved in today. Maybe you don't have any problems. Maybe you've got your act together and you don't need any help. If that is so, man, that's great! But in my experience as a pastor, I've found a lot of people really need somebody to help them. They need a community. They need people for support. If you are in that category I want you to know that we're going to have a 'Festival of Life' in our church. It's going to start on Sunday and go through Wednesday night. In the enclosed brochure there is a description of the kinds of subjects we're going to talk about. If you would like to register, just enclose $2.00 and we'll be glad to have you be a part of our 'Festival of Life.'"

Now, I would have begun looking for good people to lead a seminar on such things as marriage, how to handle divorce, teen-age problems, growing old, changing careers.

I'd want to have one on "Is the Bible True?," one on prayer, one on "What Does It Mean to Be a Christian?" And I'd book all those seminars. I would choose a Bruce Larson or a Charlie Shedd or somebody like that, who understands how to talk to secular people. I'd have a men's prayer breakfast. And I'd use that as an opportunity to get my men motivated for what was going to happen in the coming weeks; to get their friends to come. I'd have a women's luncheon and I'd meet with the young people. Everyone in the church would be informed and involved. Remember, we've got this computer letter out in that whole community—everybody is aware of our "Festival of Life." We want to make sure we take advantage of it. I'd have the guest speakers there on Sunday morning and we would start our seminars Sunday night, so that Sunday, Monday, Tuesday, and Wednesday evenings the seminars would be conducted simultaneously.

So your neighbors come and they've registered and they're in these hour-long seminars. Each seminar leader has the responsibility to deliver a seminar and sell them on coming back the next night. After that we all meet together and our featured speaker ties it together with a relational kind of message about what Jesus Christ can really mean in a person's life. That starts on Sunday and goes through Wednesday. Then I make sure that I have continuing seminars going next Sunday morning so we can register these people from that big mass of Arcadia in the "Festival of Life." I'd bring them into the seminars on Sunday morning and ultimately many people confess Christ as Saviour and Lord and become members of the church.

Now, I don't know what kind of evangelism programs you have in your church, but when I was growing up we used to spend a lot of money bringing a preacher in for a revival. I'm sure there was a time when that was a very, very fine way to conduct evangelistic outreach. My judgment today is that it's not; because the competition is more than you can handle. So you have to find innovative ways to do it. And it comes back to this whole problem of identifying where people are and then speaking to those needs. The ad agencies are spending millions finding out where the problem is. Their products aren't the solution. The Gospel, interpreted in the context of the 20th century, is the answer, but it takes a lot of hard work to put it in language a secular person can understand.

Is Christian Education Stunting Your Growth?

BY DR. KENNETH VAN WYK

Drastic attendance decline in church education programs of many mainline Protestant churches should prod those of us in leadership positions to ask a fundamental question of purpose... Why do we educate? What are we trying to accomplish? I strongly suspect that the answers to such questions, were they asked of many leaders, would indicate we are either not sure of, or not committed to, our basic purpose for Christian Education in our churches.

It has become apparent, by now, that the ills of education in the local church will not be cured by upgrading our teaching methods, by improving our printed curriculum, or by providing better classroom facilities. These are procedural considerations. They are important, but they do not get at the basic issue. Procedural matters are worthwhile when they facilitate the basic purposes of education. *If the purpose is out of focus, upgrading procedures is irrelevant.* We must first consider the basic issue of purpose.

Rachel Henderlite states that we must return even

Dr. Kenneth Van Wyk is Minister of Education at Garden Grove Community Church in Garden Grove, California.

further, to the question dealing with the nature and mission of the church, if we are to deal adequately with the issue of Christian Education:

"The crisis of education in our churches calls for stringent self-examination: for asking the most basic questions about the church's nature and mission, for assessing the congregation's current program and its present organizational patterns in the light of that nature and mission."[1]

How have we defined the church? Our heritage from the Reformation declares that the marks of the true church are: Word rightly proclaimed, sacraments purely administered, and church discipline properly exercised (Belgic Confession Article XXIX).

This definition of the church is inadequate. It does not affirm with clarity the central emphasis of the Scripture that the church is mission. A church exists by being involved in mission in much the same way that a fire exists by burning. An assessment of the historical situation indicates that the Reformation definition of the church was colored by the social and religious factors of that day.[2] That new church needed to define itself in contradistinction to the Roman Catholic Church. In the heat and turmoil of the separation from the "mother church," it is understandable that a balanced scriptural statement was not set forth.[3]

Understanding the Reformation definition of the church in light of the social and religious milieu of that day is one thing; accepting the Reformation definition as adequate for our day is something else. Because the centrality of the church as mission is not given its proper place in this ecclesiology, it has detrimental effects on the life of the church. The church has not been imbued as it should with a sense of mission. We, as the Body of Christ, have not had as high a commitment as we ought to the world for whom Christ died. Our history on the American continent is witness to this. Other religious groups, such as the sects and "isms," outdistance us badly in their zeal for communicating their ideology to the unconverted.

John Piet suggests our deficient sense of mission is due to the "static" concept of the church which we have uncriticially accepted from the Reformation:

> "One effect is that anyone who adheres rigidly to Reformation concepts of the church, stands in danger of having a stationary or static view of the church. His vantage point is some particular doctrine applicable among Christians but not operable in the world...A second effect is that Reformational definitions tend to produce what may be called a 'tennis neck' theology...Such center-line theology looks to the left and right toward other Christians. Significant as this type of theology was in the time of the Reformation, it is not the issue today. The issue today is the same as it was during the New Testament times—namely mission. As a result, the stance of the church must change. The church must look to God and to the world and find its reason for being as God's people in God's world."[4]

Our beginning point, then, is to move from a "static" concept of the church to the dynamic concept of the New Testament, where the church is portrayed as God's people in mission. The New Testament speaks of the church as the "Body of Christ" (I Cor. 12:27); Christ is set forth as our example (I Peter 2:21); His followers are to have the same mission-mindedness that was manifest in His incarnation, crucifixion and exaltation (Phil. 2:5–9). Thus Christ's Body, the church of today, is to be like Christ was during the days of His earthly ministry. His life is best characterized as a mission-centered life (Mark 10:45). His marching orders to the church make it abundantly clear that He conceived of the church as mission-oriented (Matt. 28:19, 20). Thus commitment to Christ involves commitment to Christ's mission in the world.

The question before us is simply this: "Is this concept of the church adequately reflected in the purpose and nature of Christian Education?" It is my opinion that *the stated purposes of the Christian education curricula used in most of our churches do not reflect the mission concept of the church explicitly enough.*

Planners of Christian Education in the local church must see the mission imperative of the church in sharp focus. The New Testament presents the mission imperative as a radical concept that pervades the total life of the church. We therefore cannot treat it as just another item on our list of educational objectives. It is a crucial issue that calls for the *re-orientation of our educational focus* rather than the adding of an additional purpose clause. James Smart, in a chapter appropriately titled "The Re-definition of the Goal," states the issue in compelling terms:

"The missionary situation of the Church in the twentieth century calls for a church in which each member, as they come up against the unbelieving world, will be able to bear effective witness to his faith, both in word and action. It requires Christian congregations in our communities that know they have a battle on their hands and are equipped to move into the community and find opportunities for bringing the Christian gospel to bear upon the paralyzing unbelief of men and women. In humiliation we must confess that we are not ready for the missionary situation that is upon us. The word 'mission' presently denotes an activity sponsored by us in non-Christian lands, or in distant parts of our lands, or in underprivileged sections of our city—not the occupation of ordinary church members. Our churches 'have' missions, but they are not themselves missions... The real problem is to get people in our churches to think of the Church as a mission and of themselves as missionaries... By what authority is Jesus' definition of discipleship and the whole New Testament definition of the Church ignored? Jesus did not invite men to be good characters and supporters of a religious institution, but rather to embark with Him on a mission for the redemption of the world. Those who shrank from whole-hearted participation in His mission He turned away, even though they were enthusiastic about His teaching and admirers of his person. Every believer had a ministry, a priesthood, to discharge in relation to his fellowmen, and therein lay the evangelizing power of the Early Church which made it able to conquer an Empire."[5]

If these statements are true for us today, and I strongly suspect they are, then the need of the Church is to devise an educational program geared to equip believers to invade the world of unbelief and bear witness to the Truth of the Christian faith. In other words, Christian Education needs to be task-oriented. And the task is the mission that Christ has given to His Church.

This concept of education is contrary to the commonly accepted view that says education in the local church is primarily for the purpose of Christian nurture. Larry Richards endorses such a nurture view:

"As the first concern of the Church we must retain the nurture of the Body. For this is God's design, God's strategy. This is not retreat from evangelism. Instead it is an affirmation of the evangelistic mission of the people of God. As we grow into His likeness, His love will motivate us, His concern energize us, and the evidence of His presence enable us to witness in power."[6]

These two points of view, mission versus nurture, have their roots in two basically different ecclesiologies. Thus they each represent a contrasting approach to Christian Education. In each case the purpose is different and the outcome is different. In one, the primary purpose of education is nurture. Equipping believers for the mission of the church is pushed to the background. People are urged to participate in education because it will nurture them. The church is thought of as a growth-center where believers are brought to spiritual maturity. Involvement in the mission and ministry of the church is a by-product of nurture. The assumption is that involvement in mission will come as a consequence of nurture. My experience in the church over the past years indicates that *this assumption is invalid*...such education has *not* motivated people to involvement in the church's mission. In my judgment nurture-oriented education commits the serious error of making an end out of something that is meant to be a means. By definition it is self-centered and therefore suffers from a basic introversion. It violates the example given us in Christ's teaching and life, where ministry on behalf of others is central and primary. Education that does not have this mission-orientation as its primary purpose is not conducive to church growth.

The *mission*-oriented Christian Education program holds that the primary purpose of education is to equip people for the growth and outreach of the church. Mission and ministry are in the forefront of church consciousness. Commitment to Christ's mission. Christ is Lord and He desires for His people to be involved in His redemptive plan for the world. Mission must be the motivation for education, and for every other function of the church. The church is a training-center where the people of God are equipped for their respective areas of ministry and mission. Nurture, indeed, comes as a by-product of being equipped and involved in ministry. My experience in Christian education is that a mission mentality in the church motivates people to training and produces astounding results in personal spiritual growth as well as church growth.

Growth is sought not as an end in itself, but a means to a higher end; namely, obedience to Christ and His mission mandate. Education in this posture follows the principle taught by Christ when He said, "...whoever loses his life for my sake will find it " (Matt. 16:25). In other words, the believer "finds" his life when he "loses" himself in that which is far bigger than himself, namely Christ and His mission. This kind of education is in keeping with the dynamic concept of the church portrayed in the New Testament. It is in the training of laity for the mission and ministry of Christ that churches grow.

FOOTNOTES

1. Henderlite, Rachel. *A Colloquy on Christian Education*, edited by John H. Westerhoff, III. Pilgrim Press, 1972. "Asking the Right Questions."
2. Piet, John H. *The Road Ahead: A Theology for the Church in Mission*, Eerdmans, 1970, p. 28.
3. Kraemer, Hendrick. *A Theology of the Laity*, Philadelphia: Westminster Press, 1958, p. 64.
4. Piet, John H. *The Road Ahead: A Theology for the Church in Mission*, Eerdmans, 1970, p. 28.
5. Smart, James D. *The Teaching Ministry of the Church*, Philadelphia: Westminster Press, 1954, pp. 99, 100.
6. Richards, Lawrence O. *A Theology of Christian Education*, Zondervan Publishing House, 1975, p. 56.

What Makes a Church Grow?

BY DR. O.D. EMERY

The question cannot be given a simple answer. It's like asking, "What makes a person live?" Even the most elaborate answer will likely be incomplete and inadequate.

Yet, there are unquestionably distinctives of growing churches which are likely to be lacking in most static churches. I have endeavored to synthesize the conclusions of a recent survey of 50 growing churches within the Wesleyan denomination, and the results, I believe, have value to most other congregations, as well.

Three basic areas of strength appear consistently in churches experiencing growth. These are *attitudes, leadership,* and *outreach.* Let's probe these:

ATTITUDE STRENGTHS

A good congregational climate is much more important than eloquent preaching or an attractive building. Many of those who visit a church once and never return list the common reason as "non-attractive climate." Growing churches have allowed the Holy Spirit to develop and discipline a positive and accepting attitude toward strang-

Dr. O.D. Emery is General Secretary of Church Education in the Wesleyan Church.

ers, toward non-Christians, toward other family members who may not be regular church attenders.

A growing congregation understands that God expects their church to reach the lost with the Gospel. It banishes personal excuses and fosters an honesty big enough to admit that the greatest hindrance to spreading the Good News of Jesus Christ and His Church is often our reluctance to proclaim, not the world's inclination to reject it. Donald McGavran responds to the question, "But many of these people are indifferent, are they not?" with the retort, "You know, the indifference is more often in the church than it is in the people."

We desperately need a *growth conscience*. We need to feel alarmed and uneasy over lack of fruit in spiritual harvest. Our collective church conscience should ache if we are not reproducing ourselves in converts to Christ through the church in the Holy Spirit's power. Growing churches are churches with an expectancy...an anticipation...an attitude of excitement for what God is doing through their church.

LEADERSHIP STRENGTHS

Growing churches have purposeful, goal-directed, achievement-oriented leadership. Some of this leadership must necessarily be found in the pastor. However, all growing churches have strong lay leadership, as well. These leaders are not always persons holding office in the congregation, but they are people of vision and determination, who have a sense of what God wants done through their church, and are restless to get at it. In any growing local congregation, a significant degree of momentum is discernible within the spirit of its lay leadership. This becomes the leadership potential for what God has in mind to accomplish. As the leadership nucleus seeks to know what God intends for their church, they find themselves extended in vision, humbled by grace, and committed to serve as stimuli for the entire congregational body in their efforts to be effective stewards of Christ's Great Commission.

OUTREACH STRENGTHS

In a growing church the method is never considered as important as the task. Under God, a healthy church possesses a growth conscience which prompts it to "outreach at all costs," and then finds the methods that will be most successful. A growing local church sees itself as responsible to God for the multitudes of lost people around it—and responsible for finding appropriate methods to reach these people. A growing church does not content itself to sing "Rescue the perishing, care for the dying..." as a prayer to God, but rather as instruction and challenge to itself with God's guidance, concerning its own sacred duty.

In surveying 50 of the fastest-growing Wesleyan churches, we discovered that they vary greatly in size, location, facilities, and approaches. This should be a genuine source of encouragement to all. It means that churches are growing in rural areas as well as large cities, in the South and the North, the West and the East. Growing churches are comprised of business executives as well as farmers, high-income as well as low-income laity. There are white churches as well as minority churches experiencing growth.

We also discovered, in the survey, evidence that our Wesleyan doctrine does not, in and of itself, either contribute to or hinder growth at the local church level. Growth seems to be more related to the broader issue of evangelism and the application of principles of growth by the local church constituents.

What is a Sophism?

BY CARROLL NYQUIST

It's no one's fault, really, that we in the church sometimes fit ourselves with "blinders." Our motives are sincere and our purposes are godly. But sometimes we can just get a little nearsighted. Use your "church growth eyes" to look at these ten common "blinders" which often appear when discussing church growth and church planting.

1. Different churches have different purposes.... God does not expect or intend all churches to "reach the lost." The biblical purpose of every church is to glorify God by presenting to all people of the world the Gospel of Jesus Christ in order to lead them to a personal faith. We must recognize that all persons without Christ are "lost" and we are called to bring them the "Good News."

2. In an unstable world with ever-increasing moral decay and godlessness, it is essential that we preserve our church as we know it. Our enslavement to maintaining an institution called "our church" can easily cut us off from our mission to evangelize a lost world. We are trapped into a frequently deadening commitment to maintain the *institution* of the church. All too often we "keep the machinery running" at the expense of doing what God placed us in our community to do.

Carroll Nyquist is president of Johnson-Nyquist Film Production in North-ridge, California.

3. Quality of members is better than quantity. The natural tendency for a church is to become *self-centered*. Consequently the local church must continually measure its progress quantitatively by comparing the number of unreached persons in the community with the number gathering at the church. Church growth statistics allow us to compute the effectiveness of our church's outreach to the community. If we take seriously Christ's Great Commission we must measure our progress.

4. The bigger the church...the more effective its ministry. Several medium-sized churches are generally more effective than one "super church." And smaller churches often exhibit a vitality and determination to grow, long since lost in the larger ones.

5. Establishing two or more evangelical churches in a given community is poor stewardship. The result is futile competition, wasted resources, and inevitably failure. Two churches will reach nearly twice as many "unchurched" as one. Two churches are more complementary than competitive, ministering to people of different mind sets and different cultural inclinations.

6. Only large churches should involve themselves in "church planting." As Arn and McGavran say, "Any church with its own building and pastor should consider having a daughter church." The need is pressing and the opportunity great. Mother churches often experience additional growth and vitality through the concerted effort of planting new churches.

7. American communities are "over-churched." Planting new churches is redundant. Simply add attendance and membership figures of all churches in a given community and compare it with the total population. There are few, if any, communities where a sizable proportion of the population attend church. Most communities have large segments of persons that have absolutely no significant church contact.

8. An established church will grow faster than a new church with limited resources. Just the opposite is true. Growth in existing churches and growth by planting new churches are both valid forms of growth; but the largest growth according to most denominations come from the planting of new churches.

9. Any evangelical church can effectively evangelize and disciple all persons in its community regardless of culture or economic differences. Unsaved people are sensitive to "their kinds of people." They do not relate easily to people unlike themselves. These differences need to be seriously considered in evangelism/church growth strategy.

10. Church planting is a process of developing new churches which are exact miniature replicas of the "parent church." Most lost people will not join an established church because of differences in income, ethnic background, or language. As a consequence, we must plant churches designed for the kind of persons we are trying to reach. This may also require a change in our institutional church concept. Must a church own real estate, and have a building? Or can a church meet in a home, a mobile park club room, an apartment complex recreation room and be a church? Thousands of such churches are needed for lonely, frustrated, lost men and women.

How to Find BY W. CHARLES ARN
Receptive People

A well-tested principle of church growth is that "Unchurched people are most responsive to a change in lifestyle (i.e., becoming Christians and responsible church members) during *periods of transition.*" A period of transition is a span of time in which an individual's or family's normal everyday behavior patterns are disrupted by some irregular event that requires an unfamiliar response. It is known, on the other hand, that people in a personally stable situation, with few complications or unusual interruptions, are not as often open to radical departure from their established life-styles.

Many growing churches are aware of the potential role of their church in the lives of individuals during special times of transition or need. Laity can be trained and mobilized to assist in bringing Christ's power and the fellowship of the church into such peoples' lives in a meaningful, long-term way.

For example, immediately following marriage, the couple is very much in a state of transition and open to change. After a divorce, people are also in a critical state of transition. The birth of a child is a transition period when a family will be more responsive to new life in Christ. When

Charles Arn is Editor of **CHURCH GROWTH: AMERICA** Magazine.

a person or family member is hospitalized, the individual and family are frequently open to help and healing from the local church. These and other times of transition in the lives of unchurched individuals are great opportunities for ministering to people who are in need. It is also a fact that the greater the length of time following a "transition-producing event," the less receptive the person or family will be.

The *Receptivity-Rating Scale* * on page 144 indicates 41 different events, in approximate order of their importance, that have an effect in precipitating periods of personal/family transition. The list is not exhaustive, but does cover a variety of interesting events that have been researched. The figures to the left indicate the importance of the event relative to other transition-producing events.

It is also interesting to note that events may compound on each other when an individual experiences more than one incident over a relatively short period of time. For example, someone who was just married and is also having trouble with the boss will be more receptive than if either event had occurred separately.

Additionally, the larger the number or accumulation of numbers, the longer the period of transition will last and the more intense it will be.

Congregations with "church growth eyes" properly focused on outreach know that substantial ministry and growth are available when the church can establish systems to identify periods of transition in unchurched people around them, and then reach these people, and introduce them to the caring love of Christ and fellowship of the local church. Structuring for ministry to meet needs and speedly identifying these periods of transition will open great opportunities for a local church's growth and outreach in its ministry area.

*Adapted from Holmes-Rahe Stress Test, University of Washington Medical School.

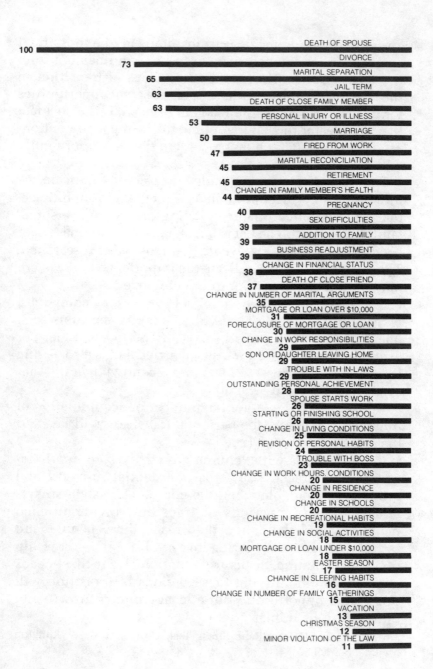

100 DEATH OF SPOUSE

73 DIVORCE

65 MARITAL SEPARATION

63 JAIL TERM

63 DEATH OF CLOSE FAMILY MEMBER

53 PERSONAL INJURY OR ILLNESS

50 MARRIAGE

47 FIRED FROM WORK

45 MARITAL RECONCILIATION

45 RETIREMENT

44 CHANGE IN FAMILY MEMBER'S HEALTH

40 PREGNANCY

39 SEX DIFFICULTIES

39 ADDITION TO FAMILY

39 BUSINESS READJUSTMENT

38 CHANGE IN FINANCIAL STATUS

37 DEATH OF CLOSE FRIEND

35 CHANGE IN NUMBER OF MARITAL ARGUMENTS

31 MORTGAGE OR LOAN OVER $10,000

30 FORECLOSURE OF MORTGAGE OR LOAN

29 CHANGE IN WORK RESPONSIBILITIES

29 SON OR DAUGHTER LEAVING HOME

29 TROUBLE WITH IN-LAWS

28 OUTSTANDING PERSONAL ACHIEVEMENT

26 SPOUSE STARTS WORK

26 STARTING OR FINISHING SCHOOL

25 CHANGE IN LIVING CONDITIONS

24 REVISION OF PERSONAL HABITS

23 TROUBLE WITH BOSS

20 CHANGE IN WORK HOURS. CONDITIONS

20 CHANGE IN RESIDENCE

20 CHANGE IN SCHOOLS

19 CHANGE IN RECREATIONAL HABITS

18 CHANGE IN SOCIAL ACTIVITIES

18 MORTGAGE OR LOAN UNDER $10,000

17 EASTER SEASON

16 CHANGE IN SLEEPING HABITS

15 CHANGE IN NUMBER OF FAMILY GATHERINGS

13 VACATION

12 CHRISTMAS SEASON

11 MINOR VIOLATION OF THE LAW

Putting Your Laymen Where They Will Do the Most Good

BY PHIL MIGLIORATTI

As pastor and enabler of a congregation, how do you organize laity for outreach? What jobs are allocated to what people? Under whom will tasks be achieved most effectively?

Sometimes church growth efforts can break down, not because of any shortcomings in the plans, but because appropriate delegation of lay responsibility to these tasks was not given adequate consideration.

Rather than nominating lay people for specific tasks on the basis of their attendance or likeliness to say "Yes," it is important for leaders to support and guide laity in finding their particular gift, talent, or special interest conducive to efficient achievement of the outreach task.

Organizational structures (boards, committees, task forces) should consider both the biblical qualifications for an assignment as well as the specific requirements of the task and all its implications. Much present lack of strength and inefficiency in goal achievement is due to mismatching people and roles. Here are three simple roles to begin our thinking:

Phil Miglioratti is on the staff of the Willow Creek Community Church, Palatine, Illinois.

ROLE ONE: VISIONARIES

These are men and women in the Body of Christ gifted with bold, creative dreams of new advances for God and His Kingdom through the church. They suggest imaginative ideas, or new alternatives to old problems. These individuals exercise their gifts in seeing new ways to meet needs in people around, but outside the church.

Our operational system must provide an environment for this necessary role to be recognized by the Body, and a method developed that insures it will be filled by the right people. The value of these positive, faith-oriented, possibility-seeing people should not be lost in a system that perpetuates business as usual.

Role One leaders are needed in every congregation. They are called upon to share God's dreams, and challenge God's people to launch out in faith and decisive action. We must be wary of the temptation to choose unqualified people for this role simply because of their elected office or personal influence.

ROLE TWO: ADMINISTRATORS

Visionary leadership is often criticized because it offers an image of what could be, without a detailed plan of how to realize it. Many groups 'solve' this problem by ignoring the role of visionary leadership altogether. A more positive solution is to first identify visionary leaders, define their task, and then correlate their ministry with individuals who provide necessary follow-up organization.

Role Two leaders are gifted in logical organizational abilities, and bring to the vision a necessary plan of action for achievement. Contributions of the Administrators are proposing alternative solutions, decision-making, developing short and long range goals, organizing strategy, setting time-lines, allocating sub-tasks, monitoring and evaluating progress.

Role Two leadership is the critical link between the

"impossible dream" and the step by step moving of the mountain. Through insightful planning, organizing, and delegating, dreams become realities.

ROLE THREE: WORKERS

A dream that has been organized into a workable plan still needs implementation to see results. Many individuals, as well as small groups within the church, should have a part in "making it happen."

Role Three leaders are those people in the Body granted the gifts and skills needed to get a job done. They work best when given training and assignments with sufficient authority to perform the task. Usually these workers are eager to invest their talent, time, and treasure sacrificially in a particular ministry, with little expectation of moving out of this role. A mistake is made when these active dependable servants are 'rewarded' for their work by 'promoting' them to Role One or Two positions.

In conclusion, it should be understood that these roles are numbered for identification and sequence, NOT for rank or value. Until each of these three leader-role groups work together, little progress is ever made. All three roles are equally critical to the success of a church's outreach endeavors.

As the gifts and strengths of lay leadership are understood and properly correlated to leadership roles, God's work and our church's major responsibility of outreach are most immediately and effectively accomplished.

Your Church and Your Leadership Style: Are They Compatible?

BY TED ENGSTROM
and EDWARD DAYTON

Let us assume that your church has begun growing and changing. A momentum for growth is developing among the laity, and the outreach programs are bringing new Christians into the church. What changes and special needs should you be aware of, as a pastor, to accommodate this growing difference in size?

First, be aware that leadership needs will change. Interestingly, few pastors have the ability to grow as rapidly as their churches. The pastor(s) must gain new abilities and be supported with strong associates who are permitted to exercise their skills, or the situation may become quickly unmanageable.

Second, plan for your own growth and the growth of your staff, in addition to the church's growth. This must include time and resources for continued education and ways of expanding your own horizons of management and

Ted Engstrom is Executive Vice President for World Vision, International, and Secretary/Treasurer of the Institute for American Church Growth.

Edward Dayton is Director of Research and Management Systems Division of World Vision, International.

organization. Someone or some group should be responsible in this area of staff growth. Rapidly growing churches should have individuals or groups specifically given the task of "pastoral development."

Third, attempt to identify and train potential lay leaders, adults as well as young adults, who will be able to lead the larger church in selected areas.

Fourth, "If you want to know something about a city, *ask someone who has been there*." If you plan to become a church with 1,000 members, seek advice from a pastor who has led a church of 1,000. Larger churches have faced most of the problems of transitioning between different sizes, and many have developed solutions to them. Check with church growth authorities and management experts who are familiar with these new types of organizational problems. Churches who tap such existing knowledge don't have to "reinvent the wheel."

Let's contrast the varying style of leadership needed by small and large churches:

Specialized skill characterizes the effective pastor of the small church, while the large church needs as a part of its leadership a *generalist* who knows how to *manage*.

The smaller church is usually headed by a *doer*, an activist, often an entrepreneur. The larger church more often needs a *planner* or thinker. Pastors of small churches tend to be *originators*, promoters of new ideas. They also tend to be *individualists*. Pastors of large churches have to select ideas from others. They are likely to be *synthesizers* and *team players*.

Small churches require *supervisory skills*. The leader needs to be close to the everyday work. Often he or she is directly involved in the actual doing. Large churches need *managers* who, while they are always involved with their staff, are attempting to work through them rather than give step-by-step direction. They need to be *delegators*.

As a consequence, pastors of small churches are involved with procedures, the "how" of things, while pastors of large churches are concerned with *policy*, the "why" dimension.

Finally, growing churches whether large or small need leadership with considerable education, experience and knowledge in evangelism/church growth; and how to apply it to their unique situation.

A Parable on BY JOHN M. DRESCHER
Fishless Fishermen

**Is a Person a Fisherman if Year after Year
He Never Catches any Fish?**

Now it came to pass that a group existed who called themselves fishermen. And lo, there were many fish in the
waters all around. In fact the whole area was surrounded
by streams and lakes filled with fish. And the fish were
hungry.

Week after week, month after month, and year after year
these, who called themselves fishermen, met in meetings
and talked about their call to fish, the abundance of fish,
and how they might go about fishing. Year after year they
carefully defined what fishing means, defended fishing as
an occupation, and declared that fishing is always to be a
primary task of fishermen.

Continually they searched for new and better methods of
fishing and for new and better definitions of fishing.
Further they said, "The fishing industry exists by fishing
as fire exists by burning." They loved slogans such as
"Fishing is the task of every fisherman," "Every fisherman
is a fisher," and "A fisherman's outpost for every fisherman's club." They sponsored special meetings called
"Fishermen's Campaigns" and "The Month for Fisher-

John M. Drescher is pastor of the Scottdale Mennonite Church, Scottdale,
Pennsylvania

men to Fish." They sponsored costly nationwide and worldwide congresses to discuss fishing and to promote fishing and hear about all the ways of fishing such as the new fishing equipment, fish calls, and whether any new bait was discovered.

These fishermen built large, beautiful buildings called "Fishing Headquarters." The plea was that everyone should be a fisherman and every fisherman should fish. One thing they didn't do, however; they didn't fish.

In addition to meeting regularly they organized a board to send out fishermen to other places where there were many fish. All the fishermen seemed to agree that what is needed is a board which could challenge fishermen to be faithful in fishing. The board was formed by those who had the great vision and courage to speak about fishing, to define fishing, and to promote the idea of fishing in far away streams and lakes where many other fish of different colors lived.

Also the board hired staffs and appointed committees and held many meetings to define fishing, to defend fishing, and to decide what new streams should be thought about. But the staff and committee members did not fish.

Large, elaborate, and expensive training centers were built whose original and primary purpose was to teach fishermen how to fish. Over the years courses were offered on the needs of fish, the nature of fish, where to find fish, the psychological reactions of fish, and how to approach and feed fish. Those who taught had doctorates in fishology. But the teachers did not fish. They only taught fishing. Year after year, after tedious training, many were graduated and were given fishing licenses. They were sent to do full-time fishing, some to distant waters which were filled with fish.

Some spent much study and travel to learn the history of fishing and to see far-away places where the founding fathers did great fishing in the centuries past. They lauded the faithful fishermen of years before who handed down the idea of fishing.

Further, the fishermen built large printing houses to publish fishing guides. Presses were kept busy day and night to produce materials solely devoted to fishing methods, equipment, and programs to arrange and to encourage meetings to talk about fishing. A speakers' bureau was also provided to schedule special speakers on the subject of fishing.

Many who felt the call to be fishermen responded. They were commissioned and sent to fish. But like the fishermen back home they never fished. Like the fishermen back home they engaged in all kinds of other occupations. They built power plants to pump water for fish and tractors to plow new waterways. They made all kinds of equipment to travel here and there to look at fish hatcheries. Some also said that they wanted to be part of the fishing party, but they felt called to furnish fishing equipment. Others felt their job was to relate to the fish in a good way so the fish would know the difference between good and bad fishermen. Others felt that simply letting the fish know they were nice, land-loving neighbors and how loving and kind they were was enough.

After one stirring meeting on "The Necessity for Fishing," one young fellow left the meeting and went fishing. The next day he reported he had caught two outstanding fish. He was honored for his excellent catch and scheduled to visit all the big meetings possible to tell how he did it. So he quit his fishing in order to have time to tell about the experience to the other fishermen. He was also placed on the Fishermen's General Board as a person having considerable experience.

Now it's true that many of the fishermen sacrificed and put up with all kinds of difficulties. Some lived near the water and bore the smell of dead fish every day. They received the ridicule of some who made fun of their fishermen's clubs and the fact that they claimed to be fishermen yet never fished. They wondered about those who felt it was of little use to attend the weekly meetings to talk about fishing. After all, were they not following the Master who said, "Follow me, and I will make you fishers of men?"

Imagine how hurt some were when one day a person suggested that those who don't catch fish were really not fishermen, no matter how much they claimed to be. Yet it did sound correct. Is a person a fisherman if year after year he never catches a fish? Is one following if he isn't fishing?

Three Spiritual Gifts a Pastor Doesn't Need

BY C. PETER WAGNER

The Gift of Pastor
The Gift of Evangelist
The Gift of Administration

An outmoded view of the pastor's role persists in a good many church circles. It is the view that the pastor is hired by the congregation to do the work of the church. The better the pastor, the less work is required of the laity. The more work the pastor can accomplish, the more secure the church can feel. It is not only an outmoded view, it is also unbiblical.

The Bible's view of the Body of Christ is one of an organism with all members functioning together. The best pastor is not the one who relieves members of their responsibilities, but the one who works at making sure each member has a responsibility and is working hard at it.

The pastor is one of many members of the Body. While he is not the head (which is reserved for Jesus), he may be something like the central nervous system which carries messages from the head to the various members of the Body. He makes sure the Body is working together in harmony. The smooth coordination of the Body uniquely depends on him.

Many lay church members do not recognize or accept this idea. While they may not expect the pastor to do

Dr. Wagner is a professor in the School of World Mission, Fuller Seminary, Pasadena, California. Adapted from Dr. Wagner's book **SPIRITUAL GIFTS AND CHURCH GROWTH** (Regal Books, 1979). Used by permission.

everything, they often expect him to do most things. This unfortunate stereotype of pastors holds that they must be accomplished public speakers, skilled counselors, biblical and theological scholars, public relations experts, administrators, social ethicists, masters of ceremony, soul winners, master teachers, funeral directors, and competent at nearly everything else except, perhaps, walking on water. This "omnicompetent" pastor is the person that hundreds of pulpit committees are searching for...and never find.

Anyone at all conversant with spiritual gifts could predict this. No one in the Body has every gift...no, not even pastors! But when this simple fact is overlooked, disappointment is right around the corner.

From this frame of reference, let's consider three spiritual gifts often thought of as requirements for a successful church growth pastor, but which can actually serve to inhibit the growth of a local church if not properly understood.

1. THE GIFT OF PASTOR

It strikes some people as odd when they first hear that a successful pastor does not need the pastoral gift. The fact is, very few senior ministers of large, growing churches do have the gift of pastor. Almost by definition, if they had the gift they wouldn't be where they are. And those who do head up large churches and still have a pastoral gift frequently find it to be a source of frustration. If not properly handled and understood, this gift often becomes a cause of non-growth.

But, what is the "pastoral gift?" *The gift of pastor is the special ability that God gives to certain members of the body of Christ to assume a long-term personal responsibility for the spiritual welfare of a group of believers.*

The word "pastor" itself is borrowed from the animal husbandry of sheep-raising.

The pastor of a group of Christians is the person responsible to Jesus, who is the Master Shepherd, for teaching, feeding, healing, unifying, helping people find their gifts, and doing whatever is necessary to see that the flock continues in faith and grows in their spiritual life.

Several biblical words are used as synonyms for pastors. The English words "elder," "presbyter," "overseer," and "bishop" all mean pastor. Because these words are used in such a variety of ways in contemporary churches, it is helpful to distinguish between the *office* of pastor and the *gift* of pastor. Most of those we call "pastors" in America are people occupying the *office* of pastor (a staff position in the church). The point is that not everyone who has the *office* of pastor needs the *gift* of pastor. Furthermore, there are many men and women with the *gift* of pastor who do not have the *office* of pastor.

As soon as we understand that the gift of pastor is not necessarily the gift your senior minister has, a vast and exciting possibility is opened for laypeople to begin exercising their gifts of pastor. In many churches the gift is not seen among laypeople simply because no one has ever looked for it. It has been assumed that when a church hires a minister and pays his salary, they are paying him to do the working of pastoring. By doing so, they may unknowingly be stunting the growth of their church.

It is helpful to think of the gift of pastor as essentially a congregational gift. Here we are using the word "congregation" in terms of the celebration-congregation-cell structure. (See *Your Church Can Grow*, Regal, chapter 7, for further discussion of this concept.) The "celebration," usually Sunday morning worship service, brings together all those who belong to the membership circle of the church. Celebration is not limited in size except by secondary and logistical considerations. When we speak of the "congregation," this refers to the smaller element(s) of the church, which bring together people in fellowship circles, and has an optimum size of 40 to 120 members. Finally, the "cell," where personal intimacy and accountability take place on a deeper level, is ideal between 8 and 12 individuals.

While the person with the *office* of pastor—the senior minister—usually leads the celebration, he does not need a pastoral gift for that function. On the other side of the spectrum, the cell group, when operating properly, draws each of the members into a mutual caring dynamic which requires only the *role* of pastor on the part of each of the members, not necessarily the gift. The spiritual gift of pastor is not particularly relevant, then, to either the church's celebration or its cell function.

It is in the intermediate structure, the congregation, where the pastoral gift becomes most relevant and finds its most appropriate expression. Churches ranging from 100 to 250 members having growth problems would do well to take a close look at this area of their church life. One of the problems might be that there is only one congregation when several are needed, and that the requirements for pastoral care have already been stretched past available resources.

What do we mean specifically? A part-time lay person with the gift of pastor, can usually handle from 8 to 15 families in his/her "flock." A well trained, full-time minister, who also has the gift of pastor, can usually handle between 50 and 100 families, depending on the development of his gift and other responsibilities of his job.

Suppose that in a large church one of the congregations (according to our previous definition) has 100 members. It may be an adult Bible class or a choir or a geographical grouping—all these and others are common structures for congregations. Chances are that the members of this congregation will not have day-to-day access to the senior minister of the church or to other staff members in a pastoral relationship.

In a situation like this, pastoral care at the congregational level becomes crucial. In a congregation of 100 members, it would be reasonable to expect that God would have given the gift of pastor to 3 or 4 of these members of the Body. They would be lay, part-time men and women responsible for the spiritual welfare of the families in their congregation. They would be responsible for this because of the spiritual gift God has given them. Some type of formal, public recognition of their gift and responsibilities would be in order. If ordination is not appropriate, then some commissioning or public consecration would be best. The point is that these gifts must be recognized, affirmed by the Body, and set into action. God has done his part in providing the gifts. The congregations then have the responsibility of using them appropriately.

Let's move from the larger church, where the gift of pastor should be operative in the various subcongregations, to smaller churches, where the membership group may be a single-congregation church. How is the growth of a church like this affected by the gift of pastor?

Here is Church A. It has 200 members and has been there for some years. The minister of the church happens to have the gift of pastor.

Here is Church B. It also has 200 members and has also plateaued. But in this case the minister does not have the gift of pastor.

The minister in Church A, because he has the gift of pastor and loves to use it, is likely to give a great deal of time to the members in visitation, meeting with groups, social activities, etc. He is probably more people-oriented than task-oriented. He typically emphasizes "relational theology" in his messages, and spends minimal time, if any, working on growth goals for the church, or planning on how they can be achieved. Actually, he may not even want the church to grow, because he is already worrying about doing an adequate job of pastoring the 200 members he has. As we said, even a full-time professional can handle only 50–100 families. Church A has reached its upper limit.

If the minister of Church A feels he does not need any help in pastoring the flock, chances are that the church will never grow any larger. No matter how often he may make public pronouncements on reaching the unchurched, being relevant to the community, and adding to the church membership, he unconsciously will not let it happen. He has no malicious intent whatsoever. His attitude grows out of a sincere desire to serve the Lord. In fact, this kind of a minister would likely feel he could do a better job of pastoring if the flock had fewer members, not more. So he cannot be expected to be enthusiastic about church growth.

How about Church B? If the person hired as pastor doesn't have the gift of pastor and tries to do the pastoral work himself, the church will most likely begin to decline over a period of two or three years. A minister without the gift of pastor can be expected to arrange his schedule to keep busy with good spiritual activities, but which leave little time for pastoral kinds of work. He may prefer to prepare expository sermons rather than visit hospitals. He may devote a great deal of time to administrative details while being available very seldom for counseling. When this is the case and the pastoral work suffers, the health of the Body is damaged, and decline is just around the corner.

But, in the final analysis, Church B has a higher potential for growth than Church A! If it dawns on the pastor of Church B that God has provided spiritual gifts to someone else in the congregation to do the pastoral work he tries to avoid, he would be elated. If someone suggested this same insight to the pastor of Church A, however, he could very well feel threatened. Because of his spiritual gift, the pastor of Church A loves pastoral work and doesn't wish to be freed to do something else. For Church B's pastor, just the opposite would happen. He would feel liberated. He could do what he enjoyed doing and still keep his job! And his lay people, with the gift of pastor, would better care for the sheep than the minister anyway—and love doing it!

An example of how this concept is functioning is Garden Grove Community Church. There Pastor Robert Schuller, like most other "superchurch" pastors, does not have the gift of pastor. If he had a tendency to lose sleep over the personal and spiritual welfare of his 9,000 members, he would long since have been taken away to a padded cell.

But one reason Garden Grove Community Church has enjoyed a steady pattern of growth over the past twenty years is that the members of the church do receive the pastoral care they need. At one time Garden Grove was a "Church B" kind of church, with 200 members and a pastor who did not have the spiritual gift of pastor. The only difference was that Rev. Schuller understood that if he was not going to be able to give the necessary pastoral care to his church members, someone else would have to. He organized a training program called the Lay Ministers Training Center, designed to help the members of his church discover their gifts, such as evangelism, hospitality, teaching, pastor, and others, and then put them to work. At the present time Garden Grove has 529 lay ministers attending to pastoral work of the church under the supervision of a staff member.

This pattern can stretch almost indefinitely. It is used by Pastor Cho Yonggi, in Seoul, Korea, in a church that has grown to over 40,000 members in less than 20 years. His 72 associate pastors and 2,600 deacons handle the pastoral work in over 2,000 home-style groups of 8–15 families each.

Two other gifts are frequently verbalized as prerequisites for the pastor of a growing church, but in reality are not really essential. They are the gifts of evangelist and of administration.

2. THE GIFT OF EVANGELIST

Church growth and church health are interrelated. Only healthy bodies grow well. Only healthy churches grow well. Stated differently, healthy churches should be expected to grow well...growth is a sign of good health. Statements such as, "Our church is losing members, but we are healthy," do not square with the biblical concept of what God expects from the Body of Christ. One of the healthy church models we have in the New Testament was the Jerusalem church following Pentecost. Among other signs of good health, the Lord was adding daily such as should be saved (Acts 2:47). If the Lord is not adding new members, something is wrong with the church.

The gift of evangelist is the special ability that God gives to certain members of the Body of Christ to share the Gospel with unbelievers in such a way that men and women become Jesus' disciples and responsible members of the Church.

One of today's great evangelists, Leighton Ford, tells how he discovered his gift in *Good News Is for Sharing.* "As a boy of sixteen," he says, "I met Billy Graham and other gifted evangelists through the Youth for Christ movement. Observing these men and women in action, both personally and publicly, I felt something stirring within me. A longing to express my faith grew. Opportunities came to speak at youth groups and then at small evangelistic occasions. People were moved to accept Christ through what I said. While I believe God has given me certain other spiritual gifts, the gift of evangelism is primary."[1]

I like the advice that Rick Yohn, pastor of the Evangelical Free Church of Fresno, California, gives to people who are anxious to learn whether they have the gift of evangelist. He asks them: (1) "Do you have a strong desire to share your faith with others? I'm not asking whether you want to see people come to Christ. Most Christians want to see a life changed. But do you personally enjoy talking to others about Christ?" And then (2) "Are you seeing results?"[2]

As we nurture laity with the gift of evangelist, we should accurately communicate the goal of effective evangelism: to bring people to a commitment to Jesus Christ and a commitment to the Body of Christ.

This statement presupposes a certain definition of evangelism which is not yet fully accepted, even by all evangelicals. It is a definition which is not satisfied with the "presence" of Christianity, which holds that a cup of cold water, given in the name of Jesus, is sufficient whether the Gospel is made clear or not.

Nor is it satisfied with adding "proclamation" to presence as an acceptable definition of evangelism. Many evangelicals still argue that biblical evangelism is accomplished when the Good News is faithfully spread, whether people become disciples of Jesus Christ or not. To report evangelistic results under this understanding means you report how many people heard the message and how many made "decisions" of one kind or another. This also is inadequate evangelism.

The definition which I believe is most helpful for church growth warmly accepts the essential need for both presence and proclamation, but holds that the evangelistic process remains incomplete unless and until the person begin evangelized has become a disciple of Jesus through a visible, active commitment to the Body of Christ.

Proclaiming the Gospel does not particularly require a spiritual gift. Nor does pastoring a growing church require the gift of evangelist. But, proclaiming the Gospel with unusual effectiveness so that new people regularly come to faith in Christ and commitment to the Body, does require supernatural help through a spiritual gift. And this gift should be actively sought and cultivated among the lay people in a local church.

Every true Christian is a witness for Jesus Christ,

whether he or she has the gift of evangelist or not. Furthermore, every Christian needs to be prepared to share his or her faith with unbelievers and lead them to Christ whenever the opportunity presents itself.

But having said this, it is time we admitted that there are many good, faithful, consecrated, mature Christian people, who are in love with Jesus Christ, but who are not, do not care to be, and for all practical purposes will not be significantly successful in evangelization in any direct way.

It is a misunderstanding of biblical teaching, in my opinion, to expect every pastor or every Christian to be sharing their faith constantly as a part of their "duty to the Master." We do not encourage our laity or staff to teach all the time or pastor others all the time or be an apostle or a missionary if they haven't been given the spiritual equipment to do the job well. So the special gift of evangelist should be seen as a key to church growth, but only when appropriate members of the Body are properly cultivated, trained, and dispatched in this vital part of building the church.

One last gift often imagined necessary to successfully pastor a growing church is that of administration.

3. THE GIFT OF ADMINISTRATION

I like to use the gift of "administration" instead of the gift of "government," as the King James Version has it in I Corinthians 12:28. The word better describes my interpretation of the gift and its place in a healthy church. A different Greek word is used in Romans 12, and is translated there as 'ruling' in King James, but could be called the gift of "leadership." In other words, I think we can distinguish between the gift of administration and the gift of leadership. A church growth pastor can get along without the gift of administration, but not without the gift of leadership. (See *Spiritual Gifts and Church Growth*, Regal, 1979, for a discussion of the gift of leadership.)

The gift of administration is the ability God gives to some members of the Body of Christ which enables them to understand clearly the immediate and long-range goals of a particular unit of the Body of Christ and to devise and execute effective plans to accomplish those goals.

The Greek word for administration is the word for "helmsman." The helmsman is the person in charge of getting the ship to its destination. That is a perfect description of the person to whom God has given the gift of administration. The helmsman stands between where the ship is, and the shortest way to get to its destination.

While the owner of the ship makes the decisions as to the purpose of the voyage, where the ship is going, and what it is going to do after it gets there, he also sees to it that a helmsman is closely monitored. The crew, on the other hand, takes orders from the helmsman and does the physical work necessary for the ship to arrive at its destination.

In this analogy, I equate the pastor of a growing church to the owner of the ship. With God's help he should know where the ship is headed and why. He needs to locate a helmsman and hire a crew. But he does not necessarily have to be or even want to be a helmsman, for the goal to be accomplished.

Pastors who do have the gift of administration can make a church organization hum. They enjoy long hours in the office, overseeing business matters of the church, relating to staff, making phone calls, closing deals, dictating letters and taking satisfaction in the total organization. But pastors who do not enjoy the above need not despair. In small churches God may have given gifts of administration to men and women who would love to exercise them as a contribution to the church. Sometimes God provides a church secretary who has the gift. In larger churches a gifted business manager is often added to the staff. For example, my senior pastor, Raymond Ortlund, is one of the majority of pastors who do not have the gift of administration. Recognizing this, he has brought Pastor Kent Tucker, who does have the gift, on the staff as Assistant to the Pastor. Kent Tucker undoubtedly has the gift of administration. In fact, he even drew up a PERT chart for his own wedding! There is no problem in our church because the senior minister does not have the gift of administration.

Pastor Ortlund is like the owner of our ship. He would not be a successful senior minister if he became the helmsman himself and shouldered the administrative responsibility for the church organization. Thousands of other successful pastors can be thanking God for the total body of Christ and for his provision of members of the body who do have the gift of administration, and would love to use it.

In conclusion, the theme of these ideas should be seen not as a negative one of hustling paid staff out of legitimate service and ministry. It is a positive theme—one of accurately seeing the congregation of believers as a vast reservoir of talent and support. The example of the body is a beautiful and accurate one. As each part functions in harmony, providing its unique and vital contribution to the functioning whole, everyone comes out a winner! The pastor, as he is relieved of duties others may do better...the laity of the church, as they learn their own value and place of ministry in the health of Christ's body...and the church as a whole, when it functions as an effective growing organism, reaching out to non-Christian men and women and incorporating them into a new world of fullness and life, as reproducing disciples of Jesus Christ. This is the potential in every local church body.

FOOTNOTES
1. Leighton Ford, *Good News Is For Sharing* (Elgin, Illinois: David C. Cook, 1977), p. 83.
2. Rick Yohn, *Discover Your Spiritual Gift and Use It* (Wheaton: Tyndale, 1974), p. 64.

Sunday Schools and BY RICHARD A. MYERS
Church Growth: Are They Related?

Is there a relationship between the number of Sunday School classes offered and total Sunday School attendance? Should a church desiring Sunday School growth increase the number of classes before it begins growing, or after? Does Sunday School attendance influence church attendance?

To begin finding answers to these questions, a group of ministers recently participated in a research experiment. The group was divided evenly, with half the pastors (each representing one church) in one group and half the pastors in the second group.

The first group was told: "If a Sunday School teacher in your church resigns this year, do not replace him/her. Instead, combine that class with another class of about the same age to make one larger class. Keep a close watch on the attendance in the new class and record what happens."

The second group of ministers was given a different set of instructions: "In every children's department with two

---

Mr. Myers is a consultant with the Religious Research Center, Indianapolis, Indiana.

or more classes, add another teacher and another class. Then reassign the existing pupils to give all classes an equal enrollment. Monitor the growth patterns of these classes for the coming year."

By the end of a year's time, an interesting trend had developed. Attendance in every combined class of the first experimental group had declined noticeably, and was now no larger than it had been at the beginning of the experiment. Result? Loss in Sunday School attendance. Something else happened, too. Very soon these churches reported changes in church membership. Not enough new people were joining the congregation to replace those who had left for one reason or another.

An interesting phenomenon also occurred in the second experimental group. By the end of the first year, all the classes that were divided had now grown back to the size of the original classes. Result? These churches reported increased total Sunday School attendance, and a subsequent increase in church membership.

The experiment provides a certain degree of evidence that the addition of classes may be an important variable to growth—Sunday School as well as church growth. Attendance in two classes will likely be larger than the attendance would have been with only one class. Eventual attendance in three classes should be larger than in just two. As the congregation provides the opportunity for more persons to be involved in meaningful group programs, attendance grows. If the congregation reduces its opportunities to serve people, it begins to shrink and the church's effectiveness in reaching people is substantially diminished. More groups mean more room for more people; fewer groups mean less room for fewer people.

But when is a group large enough to divide? And how big can a "small" group be?

Unfortunately, we cannot set a standardized numerical limit for the "right" size group. Different age groups mean different optimum sizes. (The younger the members of a group, the smaller will be the attendance before it levels off.) A rule can be formulated, however, regarding group size and attendance: "When attendance obviously plateaus, the group has reached its largest potential size under present conditions." When attendance has levelled off, another group should be started to provide a place for additional people.

One aside, in working with youth and adult groups: personal fellowship and friendship between members is more important than in younger groups. Dividing such groups may result in cutting across friendship ties, which could be counter-productive to growth. Instead, new groups should be started with people not currently in any group.

Just as the addition of more groups seems to be an important factor in reaching people and realizing Sunday School growth, certain other conditions must also be met for these new groups to function effectively. Staff, program, and building facilities must all be geared toward providing a climate and mentality for growth. Sometimes more classes cannot be added until more educational space is made available. At other times there may be ample educational space but the sanctuary is not large enough to serve the potential constituency provided by the educational program.

Such logistical requirements are important in balancing the number of groups with the number of people who can be served. A congregation loses efficiency when there are not enough people to properly manage the groups already in existence. At certain times in the growth curve, therefore, the church will be unable to effectively add more groups until the staff has been enlarged to assure efficiency of the total program.

David Womak (*Pyramid Principle of Church Growth*, Bethany, 1977) summarizes the need for staff growth to support the church's growth: "As a church [and a Sunday School] adds to its membership, it must also expand its base of organization and ministry. There is an interactive relationship between numerical growth and administrative structure to manage that growth. To put it simply, a church will not grow beyond its ability to care for its people." (See "Organizational management pyramid" below.)

ORGANIZATIONAL GROWTH

In conclusion, this study indicates that growth in both the Sunday School and the greater church will be a much more attainable goal when churches and small groups are *properly structured* to reach out, and then incorporate responsive people into the life and fellowship of the Body.

How to Reach Ethnics

BY TETSUNAO YAMAMORI

Almost half the entire population of America today consider themselves ethnics. Church leaders at various levels
are rightly voicing their concern about the ways and
means of reaching America's ethnic minorities, as more
and more churches "caught" in racial and ethnic community changes are being forced to explore their future alternatives.

Even churches in stable ethnic situations that desire to
increase their outreach effectiveness to a minority population in their area are often at a loss as to how to reach these
groupings of people.

Who are these ethnics that now make up nearly half the
population of America?

The *minority white ethnics* are descendants of the "new
immigrants" who came to America during the late 19th
and early 20th centuries from eastern and southern
Europe. The main national origin groups were Polish, Ital-
ian, Greek and Slovak. Among them were also Jewish and
Irish city dwellers. They were predominantly Roman
Catholic, although there were also some 750,000 Protes-
tants who came from central and eastern Europe. (These
white ethnic minority groups are distinguished from
white Anglo-Saxon Protestant culture groups of English
background, later Scot, Scot-Irish, and German, and even

Dr. Yamamori is consultant with the Institute For American Church Growth.

later Finn, Swede and other Northern European groups.)

The assimilation of these new white ethnic immigrants into the dominant American ethos was retarded by linguistic, religious, and value differences. They were white, but they were non-Anglo-Saxon and/or non-Protestant. Rebuffed by the dominant society, the white ethnics were forced to maintain their distinct ethnic identity. According to one estimate in 1973, "White ethnics easily number more than 40 million Americans."[1] The number is probably closer to 44 million today.

Who are the *minority nonwhite ethnics*? To this grouping belong Native Americans (800,000), Blacks (25 million), Hispanics (19 million), Japanese (951,000), Chinese (540,000), Filipinos (350,000), and other more recent arrivals from Asia. The people in this grouping all share minority status and they are all non-white, non-Anglo-Saxon, and/or non-Protestant. They are slow to assimilate into the dominant societal context.

The insight is this: To the problem of maintaining national unity in the face of racial and cultural diversities, American society has traditionally prescribed the solution as assimilation into the dominant society. This assimilationist ideology has been only partially successful, however. In the process, various stratification levels have developed with patterns of majority-minority group relations on the basis of white Anglo-Saxon Protestant cultural norms. In addition, the persistent assimilationist ideology has overshadowed the growth of cultural pluralism and the strength of each group within American society retaining its cultural and ethnic identity.

America's ethnic realities more and more betray its assimilationist ideology. Ethnic bonds have always existed among communities of people maintaining their identity through race, religion, and/or national origin. Exclusion of an ethnic group by the dominant society generally heightens that group's ethnic consciousness. Both white and nonwhite ethnics have maintained their ethnic solidarity, and particularly during the last two decades have reasserted themselves.

SIX STRATEGIC MODELS

Anglo churches attempting to reach their ethnic neighbors may find it beneficial to study the following models of ethnic evangelism. Each model has its strengths and weaknesses. Circumstances and the characteristics of ethnic neighbors are important variables in selecting one model or the other, or a combination of models.

ASSIMILATIONIST MODEL

1. *WASP Assimilationist Churches:* Assimilationist churches receive members almost entirely from people with a low intensity of "ethnic consciousness." Those in an ethnic group who are socio-economically upward in mobility tend to associate themselves with the Anglo churches and are comfortable in them. For example, Black

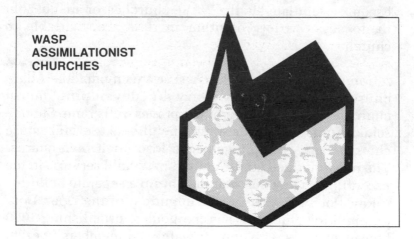

WASP ASSIMILATIONIST CHURCHES

Americans approximating WASP standards are racially black but culturally white, and are often happy in Anglo churches.

One evangelism executive, whose denomination has ethnic work in 25 language groups, made the following observation concerning their ethnic ministry:

"We are at this time experiencing significant growth in this area and have actually organized geographical conferences where the number of churches require it. We have also had some experience with an ethnic mix in inner-city churches. This, of course, is far more difficult than going the route of a homogeneous church. It is our experience that the homogeneous church is the most productive in the present social milieu. However, there are exceptions in highly-educated, high-income, racially-mixed communities. In these instances we have had some success with an inter-racial church."[2]

Assimilationist churches attract certain people in an ethnic group, but repel certain others.

IDENTIFICATIONAL MODELS

For those ethnic populations that either do not care to become assimilated in the WASP churches, or are not able to do so, a variety of other models are available to churches.

2. *Monoethnic House Churches:* In this model, the Anglo church extends its ministry by developing house churches, Bible study groups, prayer cells, and Sunday school units among its ethnic neighbors. Several house churches may group together to form their own church. The newly formed ethnic church may hold services in the parenting Anglo church or may build a separate building.

Rev. Robert Hymers, Superintendent of the Open Door Community Churches, has the goal of establishing 1000 house churches with approximately 35 members in each, as quickly as God blesses his ministry. Six years ago, he began establishing house churches in southern California. Today, as a result, there are 9 house churches, 11 local

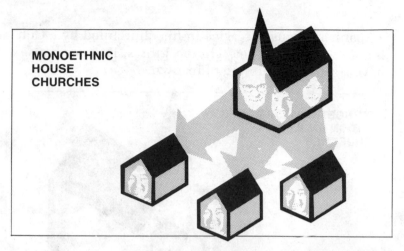

MONOETHNIC HOUSE CHURCHES

congregations which grew from house churches, and missionaries in Mexico City and London. Open Door churches include a Jewish church, a Mexican church, a Chinese church, and several ex-homosexual house churches. Hymers' method of church planting is through establishing and grouping house churches along homogeneous/ethnic units.

3. *Monoethnic Churches within Anglo Churches:* This model refers to an Anglo church starting an ethnic service within its own building. A viable mono-ethnic church emerges through reaching unchurched ethnics within the locality of the church. This model differs from the assimilationist model through its emphasis on the development of a separate monoethnic congregation within an Anglo church.

Pastor Wayne Long of Dallas, Texas saw the need to reach the Cubans in his ministry area. He discovered that there were 1,500 Cubans in the city of Dallas and 600 more in the county. These people were not worshipping in significant numbers in either Roman Catholic or Protestant churches. He discovered many of them were professionals and were quite open to the gospel. Pastor Long soon began a Spanish language service in his church led by a Cuban immigrant. As the new church grows, it may choose to have a separate building of its own.

MONOETHNIC CHURCHES WITHIN ANGLO CHURCHES

4. *Ethnically Changing Churches:* The Anglo church in a community of high ethnic inflow is experiencing changing composition of its ministry area. Ethnically changing community churches often undergo spiritual, psychological, and financial difficulties due to decreasing membership, reduced budgets, broken friendships, and fear. Some members leave the church for a church in a different location. Other members stay. Faced with a community change, the church eventually must make a choice from at least four alternatives: (a) merge with another church in the area to pool its resources, (b) disband the church, (c) stay in the community, (d) relocate to another site.

Merger or disbandment are not the best solutions from the church growth perspective. If a church decides to stay in a community, there is the important question that should be raised: "Are the people in the church committed to serve the local residents and support the church for the existence of this ministry?"

I know a pastor in San Francisco whose Anglo church has found itself surrounded by Filipinos. The community is made up of older whites, Filipinos, Latinos, and some Chinese. As the older white residents die or move, their houses come up for sale and are purchased by Filipinos.

In talking with the pastor, I have discovered several signs of hope for this church to stay in the community and serve its new neighbors effectively.

First, the Anglo pastor has a passionate desire to serve the Filipino community.

In addition, there are a few Anglos married to Filipinos among the new church members. These people, the pastor and I agreed, should be recruited to serve as beachheads for house Bible study groups.

An Anglo church member, once stationed in the Philippines and still fluent in one of the dialects, has good rapport with his Filipino clients as their mortgage insurance agent. He is an enthusiastic Christian and is a likely person to head up the task force for Filipino evangelism.

A pastor living in Hawaii has successfully trained many Filipino lay people for evangelism. The church is considering hiring one of these lay evangelists for bi-vocational ministry work in the church.

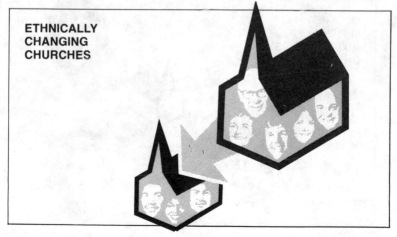

**ETHNICALLY
CHANGING
CHURCHES**

What else can a church like this do to enhance its evangelistic opportunities? The church obviously needs to develop visibility in the community as wanting to serve the new residents. Whatever means the church may use, it needs to be known as a "pro-Filipino" church. It might use one of the Filipino national holidays to invite the residents for a get-together. The church's determination to serve its new neighbors is the major ingredient necessary to function effectively as a transitional church.

A church faced with the situation of a changing community may decide to relocate. The church is where its people are, not where its building is. And so, the church may want to relocate to be closer to its members. Sound church-growth thinking, however, demands that the church leave a vital ethnic congregation behind. The church relocating should first be planting a new ethnic church.

5. *Multiethnic Mutually Autonomous Churches:* This is the model of autonomous ethnic churches cohabiting a single church building. The ethnic churches, including an Anglo congregation, all contribute to the "umbrella

MULTIETHNIC
MUTUALLY
AUTONOMOUS
CHURCHES

church" in finance, ministry, and governance. Each church has its own congregation, pastor, and lay leaders. Periodically, all the components of the umbrella church worship and engage in common ministries. Temple Baptist Church in Los Angeles approximates this model with Anglo, Korean, and Spanish congregations, as does Los Angeles First Church of the Nazarene, which includes Anglo, Filipino, Korean, and Spanish.

6. *Single/Multiple Sponsorship Monoethnic Churches:* A local ethnic church may be sponsored and supported in its early stage by a single church or group of area churches.

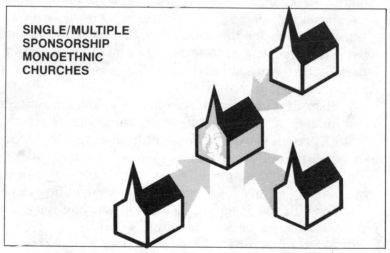

SINGLE/MULTIPLE SPONSORSHIP MONOETHNIC CHURCHES

Rev. Yoji Sato, a Japanese pastor associated with the American Baptist Church, came to America in March 1974 to serve the southern California Japanese churches in filling various pulpits. Upon taking a survey of churches in the area, he discovered that there was no Japanese church east of the El Monte and Baldwin Park areas. After much prayer, he felt called to start a Japanese church in Covina. Rev. Robert Brouwer and deacons of the First Baptist Church in Covina came to his aid in providing the place of worship. From this beginning was born the Japanese Community Church of Covina.

GUIDELINES FOR ETHNIC CHURCH GROWTH

Having considered ethnic America from evangelistic and strategic perspectives, I am optimistic about the prospect of ethnic church growth. The church in America, I am convinced, stands at the daybreak of a great ethnic in-gathering, if churches observe the following guidelines:

1. Abandon the notion that the Assimilationist approach is the only right way.

2. Focus on the goal of evangelizing, rather than Americanizing or "civilizing," the undiscipled persons in each ethnic group.

3. Acknowledge the heterogeneous nature of persons even *within each ethnic group* in that they are differentiated socio-economically, often linguistically, generationally, and geographically.

4. Recruit and train *indigenous* full-time and unpaid lay ministers to mobilize laity for ethnic evangelism.

5. Utilize the strong ethnic communal ties (friendship and kinship) to the advantage of spreading the gospel.

6. Develop para-church organizations for ethnic evangelism (i.e., missionary organizations working within America with the specific purpose of winning these unchurched persons of various ethnic groups).

7. Start numerous ethnic churches, Sunday school classes, and evangelistic home Bible study fellowships.

8. Use the indigenous (heart) language of the ethnic people as a rule.

9. Evangelize each ethnic group to its fringes.

10. Conduct research to identify the responsive as well as the resistant areas within ethnic groups and sub-groups.

11. Set immediate and long-range goals for ethnic church growth at local, judicatory, and denominational levels.

12. Pray that the Holy Spirit will empower your church to realize the lostness of every person without Christ and to act decisively for ethnic church growth.

FOOTNOTES

1. Joseph A. Ryan (ed.) *White Ethnics: Life in Working Class America.* Englewood Cliffs, NJ: Prentice-Hall, 1973, p. 22.
2. Keith Bailey, letter to the author (August 25, 1978). Dr. Bailey is V.P. for North American Ministries of the Christian and Missionary Alliance.

Finding Ethnic America

BY TETSUNAO YAMAMORI

Given America's ethnic realities, what can WASP churches do to reach their ethnic neighbors? There are basically two approaches. One is the *assimilationist* approach. It is the traditional method of Anglo churches attempting to integrate ethnic minorities into their membership.

The other approach to ethnic evangelism is called the *identificational* approach. It affirms the development of distinct monoethnic churches and missions. This approach is becoming increasingly popular and effective.

The *assimilationist* approach is most effective with people of low intensity ethnic consciousness, and is least effective with people of high intensity ethnic consciousness.

The various *identificational* models, on the other hand, are most effective in working with groups of moderate to high ethnic consciousness level.

We define 'ethnic consciousness' as the intensity of awareness of one's distinct peoplehood based on race, religion, and/or national origin.

To help identify the relative intensity of ethnic consciousness among a particular homogeneous group, and therefore establish the approach that will be most successful, consider each of the following indices. Determine a number to represent a point on the continuum which most accurately reflects each characteristic of the particular ethnic group in your ministry area.

If the general trend of the responses is toward the left end of the scales, the *assimilationist* approach to reaching this ethnic group will generally be more productive. If, however, the majority of characteristics trend toward the center or right end of the scales, research indicates that one or a combination of the *identificational* approaches to reaching this particular ethnic group will be most success-ful. Use this typology as a "snapshot" of the particular target group you are trying to reach as you begin planning strategy for church growth and effective ethnic evangelism. ▶

Left	Scale	Right
High cultural adaptability	1 — 2 — 3 — 4 — 5 — 6 — 7	Low cultural adaptability
The establishment mentality ("I am here to stay")	1 — 2 — 3 — 4 — 5 — 6 — 7	The sojourner mentality ("I plan to go home")
Weak native religious identity	1 — 2 — 3 — 4 — 5 — 6 — 7	Strong native religious identity
High aspiration to assimilate	1 — 2 — 3 — 4 — 5 — 6 — 7	Low aspiration to assimilate
Loss of contact with the community of one's own kind	1 — 2 — 3 — 4 — 5 — 6 — 7	Contact with the community of one's own kind
Non-existence of culturally bounded social organizations (clubs, community centers, associations)	1 — 2 — 3 — 4 — 5 — 6 — 7	Existence of culturally bounded social organizations
Non-existence of culturally bounded mass media (non-English newspapers, radio, TV)	1 — 2 — 3 — 4 — 5 — 6 — 7	Existence of culturally bounded mass media
Lesser social distance (attitude)	1 — 2 — 3 — 4 — 5 — 6 — 7	Greater social distance (attitude)
Disappearance of racial discrimination (behavioral)	1 — 2 — 3 — 4 — 5 — 6 — 7	Persistence of racial discrimination (behavioral)
Lack of pride in national heritage	1 — 2 — 3 — 4 — 5 — 6 — 7	Pride in national heritage
Light skin	1 — 2 — 3 — 4 — 5 — 6 — 7	Dark skin
Area with high degree of race mixing	1 — 2 — 3 — 4 — 5 — 6 — 7	Area with low degree of race mixing
Exogamous marriages common	1 — 2 — 3 — 4 — 5 — 6 — 7	Endogamous marriages common
The second, fourth or later generation	1 — 2 — 3 — 4 — 5 — 6 — 7	The immigrant generation or the third generation
Frequent change of last name	1 — 2 — 3 — 4 — 5 — 6 — 7	Pride in one's name
Upward social mobility	1 — 2 — 3 — 4 — 5 — 6 — 7	Minimal upward social mobility
Dispersion of the people in a region	1 — 2 — 3 — 4 — 5 — 6 — 7	Concentration of the people in a region
Absence of "power movements"	1 — 2 — 3 — 4 — 5 — 6 — 7	Presence of "power movements"
Low consciousness in one's national lineage	1 — 2 — 3 — 4 — 5 — 6 — 7	High consciousness in one's national lineage
Residence in a community of under 15% ethnic	1 — 2 — 3 — 4 — 5 — 6 — 7	Residence in a community over 50% ethnic

New Member Recruitment

BY DR. RAY SELLS and
DR. DONALD LaSUER

A System that Works!

"Our bodies have many parts, but the many parts make up only one body when they are all put together. So it is with the "body of Christ." I Corinthians 12:12 ff (LB)

Each church is a body—a living, dynamic, changing, interacting organism. This system includes the groups, functions, effective and ineffective actions which together make up the whole of the church. One of the most important functions of the complex system of the local church is the recruiting of new members.

Whether you realize it or not, your church is an active system engaged in locating, recruiting, and incorporating new members. It may function as an open system, as wide and embracing as an airport runway, or its welcome and entry may be as narrow as the width of a child's ruler.

Your church's new member recruiting system may be working for you or against you. But, it is always working.

Dr. Sells is Director of Congregational Growth for the Board of Discipleship, United Methodist Church.

Dr. LaSuer, former District Superintendant, is Senior Pastor at First United Methodist Church in Anderson, Indiana.

The worship, programs, events, groups, and people of your church combine to communicate a message of clear meaning to those outside the fellowship of your church.

Perhaps your new member recruitment system has been designed with careful attention. Most likely, however, it has been allowed to evolve and exist without guided attention or care. When the new member recruitment system is not planned and managed for effective outreach, it tends to develop around past purposes and values, and adopt attitudes toward newcomers that may actually be excluding persons and closing off outreach to the people you wish to reach.

This vital sub-system of your church—recruiting new members—may occasionally need to be reborn/renewed to provide an open, active, faithful response to the call of making disciples. It is useless to proclaim welcome by word when our system by deed is constricted and closed, or simply malfunctions because of our careless inattention. The challenge is to make the present church a caring and nurturing system, reaching, welcoming and assimilating new persons, adopting them as intimate, needed family members.

An excellent way to take a snap shot of the operation and function of your membership recruitment system is to complete the chart on page 187. The question is, "Who is performing these functions in your system, and how well are they being performed?"

Using this exercise in a variety of churches, we have made a variety of observations and concluded that the following statements apply to most churches:

1. Every church is a system; that system is alive and in communication with persons within its community.

2. Every church has a functioning or malfunctioning approach to recruitment of new members. The system may work for or against effectiveness, but none-the-less it is at work.

Events in New Member Recruitment System	Who is now responsible	Current procedures	How well we now succeed
Locating and listing potential new members			
Contacting, inviting, communicating with potential new members			
Guiding potential new members to programs, fellowship groups, or other points of entry			
Follow up: relating to, knowing, and nurturing			
Involving or including in a role, task, or group after uniting with the church			

3. The pastor *cannot be the system* for recruiting new persons, but rather must be the manager of the system. When the pastor becomes the system for recruiting and assimilating new members, the system will be reduced in outreach and effectiveness and be limited to the energy and success of the pastor.

4. The corporate message of the system functioning as a whole communicates more powerfully than the message of a single person or some sub-system within the church.

5. Some churches are effective in locating and reaching new persons, but as one moves toward nurturing, including, and assimilating functions, the energy level and effectiveness dramatically declines. The result is many persons whose commitment and faith is aroused but who are never given full opportunity to belong, grow, and serve.

6. Many churches do not see the church sub-systems (groups)—formal and informal—as an opportunity to include and assimilate new members. They do not challenge church school classes, sewing groups, prayer fellowships, couples groups, bowling clubs to participate in the adventure of finding and including new persons and extending to them the care and space to grow in Christ and experience their gifts.

7. The church, left to itself, will tend to serve itself. That's the normal state of affairs. The church, as a system, must be intentionally managed and directed in its attention to recruit and include new persons.

8. If new persons fail to become engaged in a *role, task,* or *group* in the life of the church, the failure is not the responsibility of the persons who have become disengaged or dropped out, but is the failure of the church.

TOWARD A CARING SYSTEM

What follows is one expression of a caring system. This monitoring and managing approach is an attempt to redirect the system and all its parts toward the needs of new persons who are identified as potential new members. This approach has developed within the framework of a program called "Keys to Growth—a Systems Approach to New Member Recruitment."

It is a description of how this approach is working at the First United Methodist Church in Anderson, Indiana, where Dr. Donald LaSuer is pastor.

The caring system carefully follows the steps necessary for an effective new member recruitment system:

1. Identification of prospective new members;
2. Profiling;
3. Initial contact;
4. Personal visit;
5. Invitation;
6. Membership training;
7. Reception into membership;
8. Assimilating and including;
9. Continuing involvement in a role, task or fellowship group.

The Committee on the Caring System carefully monitors all names received for a period of not less than one year. A field folder is kept for each person or family in order to follow their progress.

The first step is the receiving and identifying of names. First Church tries to be a careful shepherd of those who enter its sphere of influence, those whose lives are touched by the church system, as well as those who seem to be receptive to the purpose and ministry of the church.

The second step in the work of the committee is a thoughtful profiling of each person who has come to its attention. "Profiling" is a discreet listing of information known about the person: marital status, approximate age, sex, employment, geographical location, known interests, friends in the church, etc. The source from which the name is received is noted for future reference. Since approximately 85% of new persons attracted to a church come at the invitation of those already participating, profiling is not a difficult task.

The next step is to arrange for an initial contact. For instance, after profiling a family recently, the committee arranged to have a mother in the church who had a mentally retarded child visit a family new to the city with a similar situation who needed information and resources available for their child. A phone call made from a teenager to another teenager inviting him to join the church basket-

Name, address	Source, date	Preliminary analysis	1st contact assigned	1st contact completed
Mr. & Mrs. J.B. 123 Race Street (East Side)	Worship Attendance	St. John's Lutheran	Appointment in Office	✓
J.H. 4001 Robert Street (Southside)	Worship Attendance	From Kentucky	Walk-in— conversation in the Narthex	
Mr. & Mrs. C.S. 1515 Davis Pk. Dr. (South Edgewood)	Telephoned Worship Attendance	Family. Anderson Bank Church background	House Call	✓
Mr. & Mrs. T.W. 1730 Hill Street (Northwest)	Friend	Young G.M. No children	House Call	✓
Dr. & Mrs. R.F 4501 Smith Apt. A-16 (Southside)	Telephoned	Just new in town. Looking for church.	House Call	✓
Mr. & Mrs. R.J.L R.R. 2 Alexandria (North)	Friend Worship Attendance	Family New to city	House Call	✓

ball team. A member who worked in the same building expressing his pleasure that their family had attended the church last week. Sunday School classes, women's groups, etc., are given names for follow-up calls as deemed appropriate.

Often at this time the person is given information or an invitation to the Membership Orientation sessions.

Diligent attention is given to "entry points" into the church fellowship. Entry points are those areas where new

Membership packet	Mailing list	Profile	Assigned	Completed
✓	✓	Looking for a church. Choir. Grown family.	Scott Choir	✓
	✓	Family. Retarded child. Needs job. H.S. age son.	Kate Larmore	✓
✓	✓	Active in church before move. Wants S.S. class. Children in choir.	Adult	✓
✓	✓	New in town. Wants to join.	Staff Call	✓
	✓	Expecting a child. Wife from Germany Works with Deck.	Staff Call	✓
	✓	Children age 6-8-9 Just moved to town Quaker Church.	Sunday School	✓

▶

persons first experience the church, and include smaller subsystems of the church and individual members. Entry points may include the worship hour, a Sunday School class, choir, women's or men's organization, bowling teams, etc. An organizational chart of every part of the church life is diagramed in order to insure a warm welcome. By using this caring system we have discovered what existing groups need to be challenged to be more open, where groups need to be started or attitudes and

PERSON TO PERSON CALLS					
Assigned	Completed	Assigned	Completed	Assigned	Completed
Staff Call	✓				
B.B. Coach for son	✓	Youth call son: S.S.	Don met at concert	Arranged job interview	✓
Scott Choir	✓	Neighbor: ride to choir	✓	Staff Call	✓
Scott Choir	✓	Staff Call	✓		

practices changed in order to facilitate the entrance process for new persons. Coffee hours, for instance, designed for fellowship, are often seen as "clannish gathering" by new persons unless intentional action is taken by church leadership.

New persons are brought quickly into the center of the fellowship, including the decision-making groups. Every committee or task force formed is asked to include new persons in its membership. When lists are prepared for

Assigned	Completed	Invited to Orientation	Enrolled in Orientation	In Orien.	Orien. Complete
		Yes	Yes	Yes	Yes
Staff Call	✓	Yes	No		Yes
Req. a call by A.B.C.	✓	Yes	Yes	Yes	Yes
		Yes	Yes	Yes	Yes
		Yes	Yes	Yes	
		Yes	Yes	Yes	Yes

▶

Sunday lay readers of Scripture or similar tasks, new persons are included. As Lyle Schaller states: "They know they are wanted when they know they are needed. Adult new members who do not become part of a group, accept a leadership role, or become involved in a task during their first year tend to become inactive." A thorough quarterly review of every name checks the progress of inclusion in a role, task, or fellowship group. The result is a high record of participation.

Follow-up Assgn. Complete		Decision on Membership	Received	P.X. Call	Estimate of Giving
12/6/78	√	Not now			
12/10/77	√	Not now Yes	√	√	√
12/8/77	√	Yes	√	√	√
4/10/76	√	Yes	√	√	√
8/6/77	√	Yes	√	√	√

Significant results have been experienced through the use of this caring system. First, persons are valued for who they are rather than as numbers to be "taken in." Their hopes, dreams, and gifts are considered as the basis of approach, welcome, and nurture.

Secondly, through the caring system the church learns about itself. Rather than blame people for not being interested in what's being "sold," the church learns to be sensitive and respond to the people we are trying to reach.

ASSIMILATION					
Role	Task	Fellowship Group	Participation 3 month	Staff	Participation 6 month
	Choir	Asbury Sunday School Class			
	Retarded Project Team	Elective	Regular	Yes	
	S.S. Teacher. Children's Choir.	Children S.S. Alpha Omega Class Circle		Yes	Good
	Choir	Mothers' Club	Regular		Good
Nurture Council	Youth Teacher	Mothers' Club. Men's Basketball.	Regular	Yes	Not as regular
Nurture Council	S.S. Teacher. Children: Choir.				Good

▶

Also, through this, there is a careful shepherding process developed. Diligent care is taken for each person as they are included in a role, task, or fellowship group.

In evangelism we often talk of "changing" those who knock at the door of the fellowship. That's OK. But the church needs to be "changed" as well. It is the nature of all institutions—including the church—to become ingrown and self-serving. When new persons, with fresh perspective, are included into the life of the church the process of

| | | | | YEARLY CHECK-UP | |
6 month Call Assign. Compl.		Participation 9 month	Participation 12 month	Role	Task
		Excellent			
6/10/78	√	Husband only	Husband only	Officer, Mothers Club	Choir
10/10/77	√	Less regular	Same		
2/10/78	√	Less regular	Excellent	Nurture Council	Children: Choir. S.S. Teacher.

internal, as well as expansion growth, thrives. A spirit of mutual growth is developed through the use of a caring system. Caring catches on.

To develop a caring system—reaching out and caring for new persons—is a challenge. Your church system can be directed to turn its energy and resources out to new persons. It can respond to the call of God *and* become a new community with a new life, renewed mission, and new growth.

Fellowship Group	Atten-dance	Finance
Mothers' Club	Husband (Worship)	√
	Poor	?
	Excellent	√

People Are Asking...

As church growth thinking influences more people and more churches, questions arise. Dr. Win Arn, noted church growth authority and president of the Institute for American Church Growth, brings some of the answers.

Q: *What can we do to direct our officers and "pillars" in the church more toward growth?*

A: It is easy for leadership to turn inward and become preoccupied with institutional and maintenance goals. Their eyes for seeing lost people can easily develop "cataracts"—we call it "people blindness." Consider these steps for removing "cataracts":

1. Develop a clear statement of purpose—a philosophy of ministry—for your church; one that directly relates the church and its reason for existence to God's unswerving purpose—the redemption of lost mankind.

2. Translate this purpose into measurable goals...goals which become the basis for priorities, programming and organization in the church.

3. Evaluate progress on a regular basis, as it relates to achieving these goals.

4. Celebrate accomplishment. Enjoy success and achievement in reaching these goals. People are inspired and grow personally when they see tangible evidence of God's blessing in their church.

The church that takes these steps will develop a unity of purpose, a sense of accomplishment, meaningful involvement of members and, if related to God's purpose of reaching lost men and women, a growing church.

Q: *How large should a church staff be and what position should be added first?*

A: One reason many churches plateau is because of inadequate staff...insufficient laborers to bring in the harvest. Staff to train and deploy laity is essential for growth.

Concerning the size of a church staff, the following guidelines may prove helpful:

Average Attendance at Worship	Full-time Professional Staff	Part-time Professional Staff
0–225	1	
225–275	1	1
275–325	2	
325–375	2	1
375–425	3	
425–475	3	1

This pattern continues as the church grows.

The first professional staff added after the pastor should be a person in evangelism/church growth. There is no question about this! Such a person, if he knows his church growth principles and serves as an effective enabler in helping the laity use their gifts for ministry, will be blessed of God and the church will grow.

As the church grows so will the income, thereby enabling the church to add additional staff. If, however, a youth director, Christian Education director, music director, etc., is added as the first professional person after the pastor, their work is usually internal. Additional people are not reached in sufficient numbers for the budget to grow to keep the church and staff growing, and a plateaued church is often the result.

Q: *Is Church Growth a passing fad?*

A: There is always a danger that Church Growth may become just a collection of interesting ideas. But I don't believe Church Growth will disappear as a fad of the late '70 s, for four reasons:

1. Church Growth thinking finds its basic reason for existence in God's unswerving purpose—the redemption of lost mankind. When this purpose is understood and acted upon in the most strategic and effective ways, God's blessing and a growing church are to be expected.

2. A large number of dedicated Christians, both lay and clergy, are being trained in the expanding knowledge coming from the study of growing churches. These individuals are discovering that, through the application of Church Growth principles, their churches can be more successful in winning lost people to Jesus Christ and building them into the church's fellowship.

3. Church Growth thinking brings a new dimension for the church...a new perspective or frame of reference for seeing the church. Church Growth does not mean a program of evangelism, door-to-door visitation, or phone calling. It is rather a way of looking at a church, as it is obedient—or disobedient—to Christ's command to "Go and make disciples." Church Growth then develops strategy to identify the ways each church can be most effective in reaching the unchurched in its ministry area. We call this perspective, "Seeing through Church Growth Eyes."

4. Results are achieved. Pastors and people applying growth principles see results... "God gives the increase."

All of these reasons cause me to believe that in the next five, ten, twenty years, we will see unprecedented advance of the Church in America and across the world. I pray this may indeed happen.

Q: *How important is parking space to Church Growth?*

A: Parking space will not produce growth; but the absence of adequate and easy parking space can and will inhibit growth.

Q: *What is the most important element in producing growth?*

A: Different people would respond in different ways. Some might say the pastor is most important, others would say the location, still others believe the building, or program, or Sunday School is the key factor.

There is some truth in each of these. Yet, I believe the most important element in producing church growth is finding the right "mix."

I define the "mix" as "that combination of ingredients or elements of the church which together, and in the right proportions, produce effective church growth." These same ingredients, separately or in the wrong proportions, will be ineffective for evangelism/church growth. Until a church finds the right combination, its evangelism is probably not very effective.

Important parts of the ingredients that make up the "mix" are the *pastor*—How does he spend his time? What are his strengths? The *lay workers* in the church—How many are active in the church? What proportion of their time is spent in outreach? The *budget*—Where is most of the money spent? What proportion is used directly to win people to Christ and the church? The *community*—What type of people are in the church's ministry area? Has the church taken time to identify responsive people? The *strategy* to reach these people—What strategies bring results? Are the people who are won incorporated into the Body?

These are but a few of the questions that should be asked when a church seeks to find their right "mix."

The "mix" will vary from church to church...denomination to denomination...from one location to another ...from year to year. When a church finds the right "mix," they know it. How? The church grows!

But, what if a church isn't growing? It should examine the "mix," and begin adjusting and changing the proportions until the right combination is found.

So, effective growth is not so much finding the most important element as it is finding the right "mix."

Growing churches have found their "mix." Other churches can find theirs. Opportunities for evangelism and Church Growth throughout North America have never been greater...multitudes of people are winnable and can be found in the ministry area of almost every church where they have identified and developed their most effective "growth mix."

Q: *As a layman, what can I really do that will help my church grow?*

A: Here are four important things you can do...

1. *Discover and use your spiritual gifts.* The New Testament is clear in its teaching that "...each of us has been given his gift, his due portion of Christ's bounty..." "He gave gifts to men...to equip God's people for work in His service, to build up the body of Christ."

When those in the Body identify and apply their gifts, the whole Body grows. When a congregation allows its members to be "unemployed" in using their gifts, decline and lethargy are often the result. And what is true for the congregation is also true for the individual. A person who has found and is using his unique gifts is productive, fulfilled, and contributing to Body growth and development. The individual not using his gifts will be spiritually frustrated and seldom experience real personal growth.

As more and more individuals identify their gifts, have them confirmed by others in the congregation, and use their gifts in ministry, the church is immeasurably enriched and strengthened.

2. *Influence your "web" of friends and relatives.* How

do people come into a relationship with Christ and the Church?

I have asked that question to over 8,000 people in America during the last two years. The results have been strikingly consistent: 70%–90% listed the reason they came to Christ and their church as "friends" or "relatives."

Since biblical days the church has grown most effectively through these natural "webs." The fact is that church growth is directly related to present members influencing their friends and relatives, and bringing them into their church. This is a second important part you can have in your church's growth.

3. *Keep your circle open.* In every church—regardless of size—visitors and new members must be assimilated into the congregation if they are to become active and contributing members of the Body. This is most effectively done by incorporating them into small groups—a fellowship circle, task force, Bible study, etc.—where they are known personally, and feel a sense of belonging.

While many churches like to think of themselves as "friendly" and "warm," this friendliness is often shown more to each other than it is to the outsider. Give a third important gift to your church by keeping your circles open and encouraging other circles to be open to these new people.

4. *Keep before you a vision of the possibilities.* In a recent survey of pastors, the question was asked, "What is your greatest desire for your church?" The answer that appeared more than any other was: "For the lay people to have a vision for growth and to be involved in the process."

Perhaps the greatest discouragement a pastor faces is a congregation without vision: self-centered, self-satisfied, self-occupied. In board and committee decision-making, the natural tendency for a group to take the 'safe way' usually translates into little risk, little venture, and little vision.

A far more effective base is to organize the church and its components around a vision and possibilities. In the ministry area of every congregation there are numerous opportunities for effective ministry. These opportunities can be seen and seized.

Seeing the possibilities usually begins with one person, then spreads to others. Being that person in a congregation is a fourth important thing you can do to help your church grow.

Q: *Our church is doing well, buildings are adequate, we enjoy good fellowship and fine preaching. Why should we be interested in additional growth which could spoil what we presently have?*

A: Perhaps the greatest "heresy" of the 20th century is the self-centeredness of today's church. In a world where three out of four have yet to believe, in a country where 160 million or more are pagans or marginal Christians, the self-centered/self-satisfied church is really a disobedient church. Disobedient to its Lord whose express command is to "go and make disciples."

Did you realize that to effectively evangelize America, present churches must significantly expand and thousands upon thousands of new churches must be established? There is much, much work to be done. When you and your church become fully committed to people beyond your present walls, you will find unmet needs and hurting people, waiting to find new life and new hope through Christ and your church.

Q: *"Our church growth efforts seem to have failed. What do you recommend?"*

A: Churches that fail in their growth efforts usually fail first in their view of mission. Observing "casualties on the battle field" of church growth, one soon discovers that churches interested only in institutional enlargement often falter, whereas churches truly interested in reaching and winning people, making disciples, and incorporating them into the body, grow. Retrace your steps and look carefully at the biblical and theological convictions for your growth efforts. Then, identify relevant growth principles. Then from these growth principles develop a variety of methods. Identify growth restricting obstacles and remove them at all cost. Monitor these efforts to see if they are, in fact, producing growth. Don't allow a few setbacks to dampen your spirit. Remember, there is no one universal formula for every church. There are thousands of formulas and each church must find that combination of ingredients, based on their location, their pastor, their convictions, and their community that produces growth.

Q: *"Our church just celebrated its 10th birthday. Growth has not been outstanding, but not disheartening either. A suggestion was recently made to consider starting a new church 12 miles away. Any thoughts on this?"*

A: Planting a church could provide a great new focal point of commitment for your church. It is a creative way of reaching new people, extending the ministry of your church to new areas, and involving more lay members. Planting a church often unifies the mother church through a common goal and involves members who would otherwise be left out. And these are only the benefits to the parent church. New church members often find an involvement and commitment to the church and to reaching people they had not known in the older church.

Be careful, though, to make an analysis of receptivity and the kind of people your new church will be trying to reach. Study the implications of reaching these groups in the ministry area wherein the church will be located.

Effective Communication to Your Community

BY ROBERT C. SCREEN

A FRESH APPROACH TO CHURCH NEWSPAPER ADVERTISING

Let's say that your church's Communications Committee has been talking about newspaper advertising. They want to encourage young families who are not attending church to visit your church. And let's say you have a meaningful program for both children and parents and you can handle a larger group.

You haven't been happy with the way the church has used newspaper advertising in the past. You decide to look for a fresh approach.

Pictured on page 208 is one suggestion of how you might use your local newspaper to help reach the parents of young families in your community.

There are several things that help make this a good ad.

1. It does a good job of getting the *attention* of the desired audience by focusing on the safety of a child, a subject of primary concern to all parents.

2. It turns the reader's attention into *interest* by featuring one local family's feelings about participating in church activities.

3. It moves from creating interest to stimulating *desire*

Mr. Screen is an active layman who devotes part of his time to consulting with churches and church organizations.

by showing how participating in church activities as a family can help parents do what they want to do: stay closer together as a family.

4. The ad encourages the reader to take specific *action*: to visit the church next Sunday.

5. Finally, the ad communicates in language familiar to the unchurched.

Here are some additional suggestions for making your church advertising effective:

- Repeat the ad once a week (on Saturday if possible) for at least four consecutive weeks and preferably longer. Repetition is important to increase awareness of your church among the people you are trying to reach, and to motivate them to act.

- Don't place the ad on the "church page." Ask the newspaper to place the ad in a prominent place in the local family news or general news section. Suggest an outside position (instead of the inside or "gutter") and near the top of the page.

- Select the newspaper that reaches the most homes in your community at the lowest cost to you. This would usually be the local community newspaper.

- If your budget for advertising is small use a smaller ad and still repeat the same ad for several consecutive weeks.

- If you have a regular mailing to your church family, reprint the ad in the mailing and ask members to be alert for opportunities to invite young families they know to come to church with them.

- Be alert for new families visiting your church and go out of your way to make them feel welcome.

Designing an advertising program for your church involves more than designing one ad. Develop a strategy that places an ad in your local community newspaper each week throughout the year. Develop 10 to 12 different ads on different subjects and rotate them, so that each ad runs 4 or 5 times during the year. Use your newspaper ads every week as one way to inform the people in your community of your church's desire to reach out in love to them and to meet their needs.

Last Sunday morning at 8:45 Steven Screen left home!

It wasn't the first time. It happens almost every week.

You see, Steven spends Sunday morning with about 20 other kids his age at the La Canada Presbyterian Church. His parents don't let Steven go off by himself. They take him.

Steven loves every minute of it. And his mom and dad love it too. Not just because of the way Steven is growing. But because of the way the church helps the whole family stay closer together.

Maybe you should think about leaving home next Sunday morning! If you do, bring the whole family.

Sunday Morning Worship	9:00 and 10:30
Sunday School	9:00
Youth Discovery Hour	10:30
Adult Education Classes	9:00 and 10:30

La Canada Presbyterian Church • 626 Foothill Blvd. • Phone 790-6708

Discovering God's love and sharing it with others

*Feel free to use any of the ideas you wish from the ad illustrated above. There is no charge or obligation to the author of this article or *Church Growth:America*.) The ad shown has been reduced to approximately 75% of its original size.

CREATING A CLIMATE FOR GROWTH THROUGH DIRECT MAIL

One major objective of a growth-oriented church should be that all residents in its ministry area are aware of the church, its desire to help and serve them, and aware of the potential contribution the church can make in their lives.

There are two basic strategies that can be used to achieve this objective. The first, and most important, involves the active training and use of lay members in building relationships with their friends and neighbors. Leadership of the church should constantly be asking whether the people, programs, and facilities of the church are responding to the needs of the people in its community.

A second strategy to reach the above objective involves the use of mass media.

Here are some basic questions that should be discussed as a staff and as a church *before* launching an aggressive mass media program in your ministry area:

■ How do we want the community to perceive our church?
■ Have we developed an accurate assessment of the needs, attitudes, and concerns of the people we are trying to reach?
■ Do we sincerely desire to serve the needs of these people?
■ Are we willing and able to develop or expand our programs around the needs and interests of the people?
■ Is our commitment, as a church, clearly understood and supported by the congregation?

All of these questions deserve careful consideration. Your answers will serve as a valuable guideline in determining not only what you say through the mass media, but also how you say it.

Mass media you can use to say these things usually includes direct mail, newspapers, radio, and television. Here are some specific suggestions on direct mail.

Direct mail is one of the most cost-effective mass media

tools available to your church. I suggest sending a mailing to every home in your ministry area at least four times each year. Churches with a smaller budget should mail at least once or twice a year.

An annual mailing schedule might look like this:

Early Spring: A mailing sent to arrive a week or so before Easter, highlighting the Easter season.

LETTER:

Dear Friend:

If you are like most of us you probably don't mind making a new friend once in a while. Those of us who are neighbors in this area get pretty shut away from each other. Maybe you like it that way. But sometimes you may feel like sending out a test signal to see if anyone would even notice! I know I get that way occasionally.

Life is pretty much a sending out and receiving of signals, I guess. And when there isn't anybody around to listen—nobody "to tell it to"—a funny thing happens.

Maybe you know the "ghosts" that haunt your mind when it seems like nobody cares. Maybe you wrestle with anxieties—about your health, about your job, about your family, or some special friend. Maybe you wish there was somebody around to laugh with you, or to cry with you.

You'll have to overlook this kind of introduction by mail. What I would really like is to come and sit down in your living room. I'm just an ordinary man who happens to be the pastor over at the big, round brick church south of Lincoln Park. Don't let that scare you. I'm not asking you to join anything. I just thought you might like to know that I am here, and that I am available.

If you would like to make a new friend, here is one neighbor who would like to, too! You can let me know just by sending back the card I have enclosed. I'll be glad to stop by at your convenience.

Cordially yours,

George Sweeting

George Sweeting
Senior Minister

Early June: A letter highlighting summer interests and activities available to the people.

Early September: A mailing outlining back-to-school activities, new classes, and special programs.

Early December: A special holiday mailing describing holiday activities in the church.

Of course, special church programs throughout the year, especially those designed for non-Christians, are another good reason for a mailing. The focus should be on how your church wants to serve those receiving the mailing piece. Propositional language ("the wages of sin is death") and a "preachy" tone should never be used.

Nor should the emphasis of the mailing be on the church, its staff, its building, etc. Each person—their family, their special problems, their environment—is the most important thing in their life. The emphasis is on them, not you.

The mailing illustration shown on these pages, from Moody Church in Chicago, is an example of the basic elements of a good direct mail letter. Notice how the letter also illustrates the warmth and tone that is an important ingredient.

Each mailing should highlight one particular way the church desires to serve, or one particular activity that would be of general interest to people in the community. And it should give the reader an opportunity to respond. Above all, those who receive the mailing should feel that the church sincerely desires to do something for them. You might consider inviting responses in some of the following areas:

1. "Yes, I would like more information about the program you described in your mailing."
2. "Yes, I would like to participate in the program you described."
3. "I'd like to know more about special activities for...□ youth □ college □ high school □ singles □ families □ senior citizens."
4. "I have a special concern I'd like to talk to a pastor about. Please call me about setting up an appointment."
5. "Please place my name and address on your mailing list to receive your weekly bulletin and other mailings."

If you're mailing a letter, enclose a card with the response information on one side and the church mailing address on the other so all the person needs to do is fill in his or her name, address and phone number, apply a stamp, and drop the card in the mail. A card that folds once to allow the sender's name to remain confidential will be appreciated by many.

Make sure that you reply to responses within the week. Keep track of the number of responses you receive so you can compare the effectiveness of various approaches.

CAN ADVERTISING HELP YOUR CHURCH?

Three of the primary functions of the local church in today's society are:
■ to provide unchurched people with the opportunity to find a personal relationship with Jesus Christ;

- to provide an environment that facilitates the growth of an individual's personal Christian life;
- to encourage the growth of Christian fellowship and caring support between individuals in the local church.

How can advertising help the pastor, staff, and congregation more effectively reach these goals of church growth and personal growth?

First let's look at what advertising cannot do.

Advertising is not the best way to communicate the love of God to your community. Advertising is also not an effective way to motivate people to grow in their relationship with God. Nor is there any way that an advertising program can change the impressions of a visitor who actually participates in your church program... If the experience is negative, the best advertising in the world will not change his reaction.

Advertising cannot change reality. People ultimately respond to what they *experience* in your church—not to what the experience is promised to be like. Before you spend any time or effort trying to attract new people through advertising, make sure their experience in your church will be meaningful, create a positive impression, and leave them with a desire to return for more.

So what can advertising do for your church?

Basically, the function of advertising is to influence human behavior through mass communication. What advertising can do, and do very effectively, is inform the community of your desire to reach out in love, and your desire to meet their needs. Advertising can also inform the people in your community of Christ's love for them, and of the opportunity for a personal and rewarding relationship with the living God.

If these two objectives are met, an effective local church advertising program can have dramatic results on the number of people who will "try" your church by attending a special program, activity, or worship service.

Here are some basic themes that should be included in all of your church's public advertising:

- The sincere desire to be helpful in meeting the needs of the people in your community. Be as specific as possible.
- The assurance that those who come will experience love and acceptance when they visit your church or participate in church activities.
- The promise that people will find the love of God and the Word of God relevant to their needs, hurts and concerns.
- The enthusiasm of your members toward the church.
- The sense of purpose, meaning, and fulfillment that faith in Christ brings to life.

The people in your community will be motivated to visit your church when they feel there is a potential solution to their personal needs and wants. The need may be simply good biblical preaching. It may be for love and acceptance. Perhaps to provide their children with good religious training. It may be a class or seminar on how to adjust to being a single parent, how to communicate with teenagers, how to cope with drug abuse, or how to become a Christian. It may be simply to meet new friends. These are all good advertising themes. But it will almost always be positive expectation to fill an existing need that will encourage a visitor to risk entering the strange, potentially threatening new environment of your church.

Creating good advertising is a very difficult task. Millions of dollars are wasted by secular firms each year on poor advertising. Churches, also, can fall prey to ineffective stewardship of their advertising dollar. But the local church should continually seek out ways of telling the people in its community that it is ready and willing to provide a unique source of fulfillment and satisfying new life.

When churches fail, it is not a failure of the Gospel of Christ. It is failure to effectively express the love of God in word and deed. Good advertising will never replace the importance of lay people sharing their faith, inviting their friends to church, or responding in love to the opportunities around them. But advertising can help communicate the fact that, as a church and as individual Christians, you are there, ready to meet the needs of people, where they are, and provide the opportunity to experience a fresh and meaningful new life in Jesus Christ.

HOW ADVERTISING CAN HELP CHANGE ATTITUDES TOWARD THE CHURCH

Look at the challenge. We live in a society where all of our "basic" needs are met. We've developed the most sophisticated mass media communications system in the world. Day in and day out, TV, radio, newspapers and magazines constantly tell us not only what we should want out of life, but how to get it. The impact has been so great we now operate on the assumption that anything we want out of life can be satisfied by purchasing some new product or packaged experience. People are beginning to perceive their greatest "need" as having enough money to purchase that new "thing" that promises to satisfy those unfulfilled emotional desires.

No one has yet developed that ultimate purchase to provide lasting satisfaction. But there are so many options available that most people will just keep on trying until the money's gone or someone shows them another way. And that's the challenge—the mandate—for the Church.

Perhaps we can say that your church exists in your community to show people another way...to save them from themselves and from the powerful influences that compel them to look in the wrong places for meaning and fulfillment.

My contention is that churches must not only motivate and equip the people of the church to share the opportunity of faith in Christ. Churches must also use the same powerful and sophisticated communications media to clearly and visibly present the opportunity of "another way" to the people in their communities outside the church family.

Crisis energy

Did you ever face a crisis alone? That frightening moment when you wondered where you would find the strength to go on?

It's a common feeling. But it doesn't have to be so. We weren't made to face crises alone. We need the strength and support that comes from knowing that others are standing with us.

That's crisis energy.

That's love.

Sunday Morning Worship .... 9:00 and 10:30
Sunday School 9:00
Youth Discovery Hour 10:30
Adult Education Classes .... 9:00 and 10:30

La Canada Presbyterian Church • 626 Foothill Blvd. • 790-6708

DISCOVERING GOD'S LOVE AND SHARING IT WITH OTHERS

When we use the media, we should not condemn the people we are reaching or the products, services, or companies promising the moon for $24.95. That only results in guilt and alienation. We must truthfully portray the unique biblical characteristics of the Church and the Christian faith in an attractive manner without manipulating people or offering a cheap grace. We can try to let our light shine.

The ad shown on page 216 is an attempt to highlight one meaningful uniqueness of the Christian faith and Christian fellowship. The headline was written to take advantage of the current national preoccupation with energy. To make an impact, a concept like this should be repeated several times over several weeks through different media like newspaper, direct-mail, and perhaps radio in some communities. Your church is free to adapt this ad for your own use.

SHAPING COMMUNITY ATTITUDES

What would you like the people in your community to think about your church? How would they acquire the desired attitudes if they have never participated in church activities? It's up to you and your congregation. Your members will be the major force in shaping the impressions the rest of the community has toward your church.

But few people in your congregation see the total picture like you do. Most of the people, when asked about their church, will mention the part of church life that is most meaningful to them. And this will not necessarily be the area most interesting to someone else. Your member's view might not accurately express the total perspective.

One way to directly influence the attitudes and opinions of the people in your community is to mail a story of your church life directly to their homes.

First, you will want to determine what you want the community to think about your church. Here are some suggestions. (You'll want to add some additional thoughts that express the uniqueness of your church and the particular type of community in which it exists.)

- A friendly place with friendly people
- Very open and accepting of others
- Serving us (the community)
- Caring and loving
- Sincere
- Relevant and meaningful
- Alive, active happy people
- People I know and respect

An effective format for such communication is the "tabloid" newspaper. Usually four or eight pages in length, a tabloid can provide an overview of the total church program in words and pictures. Here are some suggestions for creating an effective "tabloid" newspaper for your community:

Write all copy with the unchurched person in mind. They won't understand religious language and church jargon, and it will probably turn them off.

Use lots of photos; at least 40% of the total space. Put a descriptive caption under each photo.

Feature the personal experiences of members whose lives are being touched by God through the church. Let them tell in their own words, what it means to be a member of the community of faith.

Highlight ministries and programs of the church that would appeal to a large proportion of the readers (children, youth programs, singles ministry, young marrieds, elderly programs, etc.) Especially highlight these areas in the photos.

Show how the church is serving the community.

Cover every major area of church activity.

Have the pastor write a short column communicating the church's desire to minister to and serve the needs of people in the community.

Strive to show the relevance and meaning of faith in Jesus Christ to life today.

The eight page tabloid shown on page 218 is produced by an all volunteer task force of church members. Once each year it is produced especially for the community and three times a year for the church members. Here's what it costs to produce 7000 copies:

Copywriting, editing, typing................volunteers
Photography ....volunteers
Photo processing $15.00

Layout and Artwork .... volunteers
Typesetting and printing $500
Mailing list cost (6,600 names) $81.25
Postage (non-profit, bulk rate $175.00

   Total Cost $771.25

There are many other ways to influence attitudes and help create a climate in your community that enables your church to become more effective in reaching and serving others. I encourage you to develop a communications strategy for your church that reaches everyone in your community that God has called you to serve.

The contents of this book are reprinted from the following issues of CHURCH GROWTH:AMERICA magazine: